Marketing Your Mind

PALM TREE
PUBLICATIONS

Marketing Your Mind

Turning Your Ideas Into Marketable Media

Wendy K. Walters

Branding Consultant & Entrepreneur

Marketing Your Mind
Turning Your Ideas Into Marketable Media

Editor: Philip R. Byler

Printed in the USA

Library of Congress Control Number: 2011933218

ISBN: 978-0-9846311-6-2

Prepared for Publication By

PUBLICATIONS

Palm Tree Publications is a Division of Palm Tree Productions
www.palmtreeproductions.com
PO BOX 122 | KELLER, TX | 76244

To Contact the Author:

www.PalmTreeProductions.com

www.WendyKWalters.com

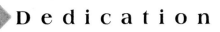 

Dedication

To my father—the most consistent "red pen" in my life:

You gave me a love of language and instilled a passion for the written word. You taught me to express my ideas on paper and you were tireless in marking them for revision. You taught me to reach for excellence in communication.

Your life demonstrates integrity and you have taught me to remain true to myself and my principles no matter the cost. Your "red pen" shaped my character as much as it did my writing. It is my great privilege to be your daughter.

This book is dedicated to you.

I'll love you for always ...

Marketing Your Mind

Endorsements

For over 30 years as a senior manager with both UniLever and the Coca-Cola Company, I have seen many new innovative products, branding, and marketing ideas succeed and fail as they go to market. The success rate is about 10 - 15%. Wendy will help you get it right! I highly recommend *Marketing Your Mind* for those coming on the scene with a new product to a new market and those who need to re-brand themselves in today's economy. Wendy has helped me get my book and message of "focus" to the masses with her creative thinking and expertise of how to brand oneself to see greater levels of success.

Ed Turose
The Focus Coach | www.focuscoach4u.com

The amount of practical wisdom that equips, guides, and inspires in *Marketing Your Mind* is remarkable. These ideas are not untested theory but something Palm Tree Productions practices every day. Anyone with a vision or an undeveloped idea will be well served through the powerful information presented in this book.

Tim Taylor, *Commander USNR (ret)*
President, Kingdom League International | Renton, Washington

From the moment I read the opening words, I knew we had something fresh, innovative and practical—in all areas Wendy excels! Ready to bring your product ideas to market? Wendy is your indispensible resource for success!

Brenda Byers-Im
Business & Success Coach | Founder IMPaX WORLD

Marketing Your Mind shares Wendy's professional insights and practical experience gained through helping many people discover what makes them and their idea marketable. Wendy shows you how to "connect" what is in your heart and mind and share it with people who have the same interest and passions—making success attainable.

Dr. John Polis
President, Revival Fellowship International, Inc.
Founder, Faith Church International and John Polis Ministries

For anyone desiring to take an idea, innovation, book concept, business, or ministry to a larger audience, *Marketing Your Mind* is an indispensible companion guide. *Marketing Your Mind* contains dozens of invaluable keys to unlock the mysteries of building a successful brand, writing your book, and developing successful marketing strategies for your enterprise. I can only say that what she's written in this book is, like her media company, a potent and rich resource.

Bob Englehardt
Author, Speaker, Radio Host

Wendy Walters is a consummate professional who is in an elite class. My own experience with Wendy as a client is that she is a tireless prayer warrior, an encouraging coach, an outstanding editor and wordsmith, exceptional formatter and graphic designer, a loyal friend, fierce competitor, and can often move deadlines and prices in the printing world with a single phone call. She goes the extra mile and delivers "WOW!"

Dr. Bruce Cook, *Author | Speaker*
President, VentureAdvisers, Inc. and Kingdom House Publishing
www.kingdomhousepublishing.com

Contents

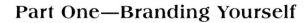

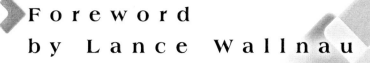

Foreword
by Lance Wallnau

We live in an age when we are bombarded with messages. The advertising of a product is reduced to a mere thirty second impression.

It's a "scratch and sniff" world where products, people, and discussions of global importance are reduced to media sound bites. Like it or not, he who tells the better story—wins! We flip through 300 channels and turn off the TV because "nothing is on." In a world surrounded by stimulus, you really need to stand out from the crowd to make your presence known.

That's the bad part. The good part is that the new era of social media, publishing, and technology gives you space to compete with anyone. You can be the expert in your niche and dominate your sandbox—*if* you are really good and know how to position yourself and your message. In a real sense YOU are the product. You are your own personal brand. When people meet you they meet an idea, a story, a potential transaction.

They ask themselves if you fit into their world and how you can benefit them in their journey. They are wondering if they want to invest more time in knowing you. I know, you and I may not want to be categorized this way but that's the way it has been for thousands of years. It has only been made more intense in the 21st century. But take heart, even the savvy Apostle Paul told his audience in Corinth, "you are an epistle, known and read of all men." The question is this: what are people seeing when they read you?

That's where Wendy Walters comes into my life and yours. She "gets it." Like few others, she can take you by the hand and walk you through the maze of distinctions that ultimately lead you through to the other side—looking better, sharper, and with no loss of your originality. With Wendy you will be able to market who you are and what makes you distinct in a cacophony of voices. Read this book with a pen in hand, mark it up, and take action. That's what I am doing.

You have a book inside you that needs to be written, a product that needs to be packaged, branded, and sold. You have an idea inside you that can make you money while changing someone's life for the better.

Wendy is really amazing! She is the person to go to so you can sort through these decisions and bring to birth the gift you were born to give the world.

Lance Wallnau
President, LanceLearning
www.LanceLearning.com

Acknowledgements

*My heart is filled with gratitude for all who are part
of my journey. I am who I am because of you.*

*To God—it is Your touch that shapes me, inspires
me, and gives me a purpose to live.*

*To my husband, Todd—you always believe the best about me
and encourage me to "go for it" ... whatever "it" may be.*

*To my children: Kathryn, Emily, and Joshua—my life is perfect
because you are in it. You fill my days with joy and meaning!*

*To my mother, Judy—my biggest fan. You support me through
good times and bad. Your sacrifice for my good is an inspiration.*

*To my father, Philip—for challenging me and pushing
me to go beyond whatever I think is possible.*

*To my mentors—for blazing the trail before me and
teaching me what you learned by experience.*

*To my friends—for your love and laughter, support and prayers.
My life is infinitely richer because it is shared with you.*

When we become more fully aware that our success is due in large measure to the loyalty, helpfulness, and encouragement we have received from others, our desire grows to pass on similar gifts. Gratitude spurs us on to prove ourselves worthy of what others have done for us. The spirit of gratitude is a powerful energizer.

— Wilferd A. Peterson

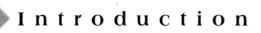 

Introduction

I deas, innovations, inspirations—all sorts of thoughts ramble through your subconscious mind. They come. They go. Sometimes the good ones—the really good ones—stick around, looking for expression. These are the kinds of ideas that can shape your future and change your life.

Ideas are my business. I am focused on turning really great ideas into tangible expressions that are not only powerful, but marketable as well. Ideas are the foundation of progress. They are the root system of invention. Ideas that are translated into useful information allow others to comprehend them, apply them, and build from them.

A book, a song, a recipe, and an engineering blueprint all have one thing in common. They began in someone's mind. Business ideas, great movies, inspirational sermons, and rousing speeches all originate in the mind. They may be awakened by someone else's idea, by a piece of music or work of art. They could be stirred by nature or prompted by the very best kind of inspiration—when the Creator Himself whispers in your spirit and stirs the Divine within. Ideas are developed through a progression of thought, but only if time and focus are dedicated to actually process those ideas into conclusions.

1

Ultimately ideas must be committed to a physical expression—a spoken or written word, a canvas, a drawing board, or a model.

Many people fail in life, not for lack of ability or brains or even courage, but simply because they have never organized their energies around a goal.
—Elbert Hubbard

Ideas turned into solid communication can be transformed into the products and services, programs and structures that define our world and shape our culture. I help people like you shape your ideas and inspirations into tangible property.

Bringing your ideas to market is not meant to be a "one man job." It much more accurately resembles a relay race. Runners line up along a predetermined route. Each member of a team must wait for the previous runner to arrive. That runner passes a baton to the next. The next person races off with pure focus, dedicated to their specific task to move the team ever closer to the goal. Only when the final runner breaks the tape and crosses the finish line is the race complete.

When you do cross that finish line and your ideas become a book or some other form of media, they are protected by specific laws. This information is identified as intellectual property and it can be extremely valuable. Beyond the fundamental value of the content, it is also capable of creating streams of revenue as a marketable product that was birthed in your mind.

What is intellectual property?

Intellectual property, in simple terms, is the collection of ideas, innovations, and inventions you have created and to which you have legal rights. Those unique and powerful ideas are valuable and they belong to you. You have a legitimate right to convert them into marketable merchandise and receive the income they generate.

You are the captain of your team, the initial and primary runner. When you do write your book, develop your seminar, or create your coaching program, a whole team waits along the route with anticipation, ready to run their leg of the race and bring your project through to the finish line.

Your story is unique. Your experience and expertise are distinctive. The ideas floating inside your head have remarkable worth. They are just waiting to be dug out, shaped, polished, and marketed. That is what this book is about: digging the precious stones of your intellect out of your mind, shaping them into a tangible communication, producing it in a marketable format, and selling it for profit—marketing your mind.

Marketing Your Mind

Part One

Branding Yourself

Products are made in the factory,
but brands are created in the mind.

—Walter Landor

Marketing Your Mind

Chapter One

Define Your Brand

In this age of over-information, misinformation, and Google® records, your identity can take a beating and often does. Who are you? What do you stand for? What are your preferences? The answers to these, and a whole lot of other questions about you, reveal the real you. But, is the real you coming through?

Being able to present yourself as yourself and your business as your business is a significant thing. Most people don't craft the presentation. They live with the information that is available about them and hope it won't do them any damage. Sometimes this works, sometimes not. But the problem of incorrect or incomplete information can be addressed with proper branding.

Have you given serious thought to the concept of brand identification? How about personal branding? With the inception of the Internet and the global accessibility of even

7

the smallest of businesses, the need for a quality brand has become a significant challenge. Creating such a brand usually requires the help of a professional, someone who understands how to integrate your personality and ideology with graphic symbols and carefully crafted language. Ultimately, your brand has a lot to say about you.

Why Does a Brand Matter?

Your brand is the imprint of your identity. It is the visible representation of you, your ideas, and your professional persona. Your brand expresses who you are. The purpose of a brand is **Your brand is the imprint of your identity.** to manage your name, even if you don't own a business. Furthermore, your brand connects you to your customers. It is more than a graphic symbol. It is everything that symbol represents. It is the person and company behind that symbol.

A brand is what your customers say it is!
—Erik Hansen

You need your brand to touch the hearts and minds of your customers and prospects. After all, your brand is not merely your ideas about yourself. Your brand is the sum total of your customers' experiences and perceptions as well. You want to influence as many of their perceptions as possible.

Define Your Brand

Your brand is the foundational piece of your marketing communication, one you do not and should not want to be without. A strong branding strategy communicates a message that draws the target audience you want to attract. A brand communicates confidence in what you offer and highlights the differences between you and your competitors.

People have a "brand experience" whenever they interact with you, your business, or your ministry. That branding perception extends to interaction with your employees and representatives as well as experiences linked to the products and services offered. It is in your best interest to carefully manage every aspect of the brand experience.

Your brand represents the totality of your company and its business. Your brand is made up of the sum total of the good, the bad, the ugly, and the off-strategy attached to you and your company.

Your brand is both your best and your worst product. Your brand is your most unfavorable employee as well as your top producer. Your "on-hold" music and the demeanor of your company's receptionist are attached to your brand. When a valued client or prospect is responded to courteously and promptly, or if that client is placed on hold indefinitely, your brand is affected.

Your brand encompasses the carefully crafted comments delivered by the Chief Executive Officer. It is also the carelessly dropped complaints in earshot of customers. Your brand is expressed through written, audio, and visual communication. It passes through emotional filters which are common to every human being. Practically anything can be interpreted in practically any way. And is.

You must pay attention and manage the image and the actual experience others have when they interact with your brand. You want to make this encounter positive.

What's in a Name?

Whether or not you look to the Bible for spiritual guidance and strength, it offers uncommonly good sense about the benefit of a good name. It offers a wealth of insight regarding the value of your name. It speaks to favor. It speaks to wealth and success. It addresses your reputation and the graciousness of your spirit. So, what's in a name? The answers I've found to that question are: favor, a sterling reputation, and a gracious spirit.

> *A **good name** is rather to be chosen than great riches, and loving **favor** rather than silver and gold.[1]*

> *A **sterling reputation** is better than striking it rich; a **gracious spirit** is better than money in the bank.[2]*

Favor

People who experience the force of favor find doors open to them that are closed to others. They seem to find opportunity for influence and advancement in any situation. They flourish and succeed even in the face of adversity.

In the Bible, people who demonstrated uncompromising faithfulness to God experienced this force of favor and were able to accomplish remarkable things. Abraham, Noah, Joseph, Esther, Nehemiah, and David are just a few examples. You too can experience this dynamic force of favor, though it is not something that can be manufactured or bought. Favor with God and with men comes to those with impeccable character and integrity. This attracts favor.

The bottom line for business success is profitability. Altruism is a fine thing. In fact, I sincerely believe that when we are blessed, it is so that we can be a blessing to others.[3] But even non-profit companies and ministries require operating funds to survive. Accomplishing a vision and achieving the goals of your mission takes money to handle the logistics. Creating multiple streams of income allows you greater freedom to pursue your destiny.

> **The bottom line for business success is profitability.**

The force of favor is a powerful reason to protect your name and your brand. When your name gets tarnished, whether because of your indiscretion or through circumstances beyond your control, your success suffers. A wise individual will do everything possible to protect their name and that of their company or their ministry.

A Sterling Reputation

Synonyms for sterling are: authentic, genuine, exceptional, and first-rate. Who would not want those attached to their

11

reputation? To be kind—really kind, is a quality that shapes a person's reputation more than almost any other.

*Never let **loyalty** and **kindness** get away from you! Wear them like a necklace; write them deep within your heart. Then you will **find favor** with both God and people, and you will **gain a good reputation**.*[4]

Notice again the theme of favor and a good reputation. In the verse above this comes from loyalty and kindness.

When your name becomes synonymous with your brand, and your name is of the best reputation, your brand rises to the forefront in people's minds. When they purpose to employ your service or engage in your market segment, you are first on the list of companies or people they will contact. People want to do business with someone who is kind, trustworthy, and has a sterling reputation backed by competence, integrity, and skill.

A brand for a company is like a reputation for a person.
—**Jeff Bezos (CEO, Amazon.com)**

A Gracious Spirit

Each day you face new challenges and opportunities. Sometimes those are exciting and stimulating. At other times, they are filled with apprehension and stress. When your name is a good name, it means you are authentic. When obstacles and challenges arise, you will be unfazed. You will be relaxed and unperturbed. When your life is congruent with your values, making the right decisions is easier.

"No shuffling or stumbling around for this one, but a **sterling** *and* **solid** *and* **lasting reputation**. *Unfazed by rumor and gossip, heart ready, trusting in GOD, spirit firm, unperturbed, ever blessed, relaxed among enemies...*[5]

Having a gracious spirit may not seem like a quality sought after in a CEO. Having this quality associated with your name and your brand does not mean that you cannot be tough or competitive. It does mean that others are important to you. It means that you are not self-centered and therefore your company's mission is larger than making money to benefit a few individuals. I have encountered some very successful businessmen who are among the most gracious souls I know. When I am with them I find a soothing, strengthening awareness of their power to succeed.

To summarize, creating your brand begins with your name. Your brand is built on your reputation. A catchy slogan and a cool logo are no substitute for the true character, integrity, and core competencies of who you are. To create a solid brand, you must begin by having a good name.

Marketing Your Mind

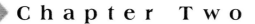

Chapter Two

Focus Your Brand

Creating a brand and adjusting a brand are very similar processes. Creating a brand requires you to start from scratch and build from the ground up. If you already have some branding in place, you should consider adjusting your brand when it is (1) unremarkable in graphic quality and visual communication, (2) poor in reputation and customer acceptance, or (3) outmoded, outdated, and out of touch with your customer base or core message.

Whatever the reason for pursuing brand development, the same basic questions must be asked and answered. The principles are the same in each case, with one exception. A new brand will not change bad business principles or habits, unprincipled or dishonest employees, a lack of integrity, or deceitful business practices. Any new brand will soon be sullied by a failure to evaluate and refurbish the internal life of an organization as well.

Creating your brand will require you to address the following questions.

1. **What products and/or services do you offer?**

   You must identify the product or service and define its qualities. This sets the tone for your brand, because it will categorize you within a particular industry group and begin to provide direction for logo design.

2. **What is the purpose of your products or the usefulness of your services?**

   Purpose and usefulness communicate the contribution of your company or your individuality and your determination to live up to the promise it projects.

3. **What are the core values of your company?**

   Core values lie at the heart of a company's mission and business style. Your branding should focus on what matters most to you. Core values should be clear to others. There should be no mistake about WHY you do what you do. Branding will make sure these values are clearly identified and elevated in the perception of others.

4. **What are your core competencies?**

   What you do and do well rises to the surface as a target value in communicating your professional image. Rather than trying to be everything to everybody, it is best to focus on what you do best. This allows for mastery and a level of excellence that will set you apart from your competition. Your overall brand must highlight those competencies in a way that causes people to take notice.

5. What is the mission of your company?

Like core values, company mission (or personal purpose) provides the branding consultant insight into what must be projected in the overall brand. Through the branding process, a clear mission message will emerge that provides the steady drumbeat that all communication about your brand must sync with.

6. Who is your target market?

A specific segment of the market should be considered when a brand is put together. Very few products and services are meant for the entire public. Most products target groups in unique demographics. Target market groups can differ widely in terms of financial strength, cultural preferences, educational level, occupation, age, and even gender. Knowing who you plan to target is very important. It will maximize your efforts and minimize your marketing budget.

7. Who do your products and services attract?

Even within a niche group, people's tastes vary widely. Your brand needs to appeal to the most significant set in your target audience.

8. What does your brand promise?

Promises on which you cannot deliver must be eliminated from your brand. If your brand promises a product or a service you cannot produce, people will quickly abandon your brand in favor of another. It is better to under-promise and over-deliver than to fall short of meeting stated objectives with your clients.

9. What message does your tagline send to your prospects?

Tagline is a media industry word for that unique statement accompanying a logo in the brand development. For example: *Palm Tree Productions — Possibilities,* or *BMW — The Ultimate Driving Machine,* or *Nike — Just do it!*

Having an honest and powerful tagline is important, especially when branding a company. A personal tagline is not necessary, though a personal value or an important aspect of one's mission or purpose could be used. For example, I sign all my correspondence, "Committed to your success." This is at the heart of what I do and part of my personal mission. This tagline sums that up nicely. My husband signs everything, "I can, I will, and I'm able." He is a problem solver and solution seeker. His personal tagline reflects this core value. Sure, "Sincerely," or "Respectfully," will do—but using a personal tagline is an opportunity to be remembered.

Your brand is a visual and verbal promise of the value your customers will receive. This should be strong and clear. Whenever possible, I try to exceed expectations. In other words, I like to give people more than they expect, and be able to deliver greater than my communications indicate. It surprises them and blesses them. When it is time to choose again, they remember this positive experience and will return to me with their next project.

Your premium brand had better be delivering something special, or it's not going to get the business.
—Warren Buffett

10. Where is our "Blue Ocean?"

Perhaps I should explain. The terms "Blue Ocean" and "Red Ocean" have become standard terminology by which business people identify the kind of market they are trying to reach. For instance, if you're an Internet marketer, or are in direct sales (like a multi-level marketing business), or if you're a network marketer selling on Ebay® or Craig's List®, you are said to be fishing in a Red Ocean. The Red Ocean has been overrun with other anglers, all fishing in the same waters to catch the same fish.

A Blue Ocean is a fishing ground that is uncontested. You are the only one fishing in that market and the opportunity for rapid growth and profitability is huge. It is often a new or unique market. But should you become successful, you will soon attract other fishermen to come into your part of the ocean.

So ask yourself, "Do we have a Blue Ocean?" Or, are you offering virtually the same product or service to the same people everyone else is trying to reach? Trust me, Blue Ocean is a calmer sea and a more peaceful path to success. Being different can be awesome.

One avenue to finding Blue Ocean is to be unexpected. Avoid duplicating everyone else's formula even if it is successful. It isn't necessary to re-invent the wheel, just innovate it! Find a way to make the wheel better, more attractive, more desirable, more useful, or a better value.

> *"If you can, be first. If you can't be first,*
> *create a new category in which you can be first."*
> **—Al Ries & Jack Trout**

11. What can we improve?

People who are treated with courtesy and sincerity appreciate it. Is there too much chatter in your sales proposals? Too little explanation? Hard sell that is offensive? All these characteristics can have a negative impact on your brand. Consider upgrading weak areas in your organization that will affect the future acceptance of your brand.

Pay attention to comments and suggestions, particularly of prospective clientele. That does not mean you should accept or adopt a change with every criticism. However, when you hear continuing commentary that reveals strengths or weaknesses in your company, it is an opportunity to grow and improve.

Capitalizing on strengths can be greatly beneficial, while modifying areas of weakness can produce new strengths. Knowing what these are in the branding process provides insight into the image you are seeking to communicate.

Objectives That a Good Brand Will Achieve

1. Your brand must deliver your message clearly.

People will not take the time to study your company or ministry in depth unless they are attracted to it. While your entire brand will not be evaluated at first glance, your entire brand will be represented by your logo, your tag line, and your "up-front" communications.

2. Your brand must confirm your credibility.

What you say about yourself will either be true or it will be a "snow job." It will not take long for people to figure out which it is. Be sure that your brand projects a true and verifiable image. The long range results are worth any preliminary effort. Distance yourself from the temptation to project your unreachable expectations as a part of your brand. If you reach a higher level of success you can always upgrade your brand and include the improvements.

3. **Your brand connects your targeted prospects emotionally to your company.**

   Even when they have not yet become customers, targeted prospects notice your branding—even when they are not aware they are paying attention. If other suppliers fail or fall short, you are now a better option. Your brand gives them choices in the process to achieve their own goals. Repeated attempts to reach a target audience need to project a consistent and confident perception of your company.

4. **Your brand motivates the buyer to use your product.**

   Today, many brands are projected on consumer items. Sporting goods, automobiles, windows in businesses, give away items, and all sorts of other paraphernalia are imprinted with logos and taglines. A quality brand attracts attention and people are motivated to utilize those brands.

5. **Your brand solidifies user loyalty.**

   People identify with a winner. If perception of your brand is positive, people are attracted to it. This is why people drink Gatorade® or wear a Rolex® watch. Positive brand identification guides purchasing decisions. Over time your brand becomes a familiar friend that can be trusted and depended on.

6. Your brand protects your intellectual property.

The US Patent and Trademark Office identifies a trademark as *"any word, name, symbol, or device, or any combination, used, or intended to be used, in commerce to identify and distinguish the goods of one manufacturer or seller from goods manufactured or sold by others, and to indicate the source of the goods. In short, a trademark is a brand name."*

A trademark that is not legally registered is designated by the symbol ™. A registered trademark is designated by the ® symbol. A service mark is used to identify services of intangible activities (rather than products). A service mark is designated by the ᔆᴹ symbol.

The owner of a trademark can commence legal proceedings for trademark infringement and registration of the trademark is not necessarily required. However an unregistered mark may have limited protection. A registered trademark has stronger defense.

A trademark should not be confused with copyright. According to the US Copyright Office FAQ, copyright *"protects original works of authorship including literary, dramatic, musical, and artistic works such as poetry, novels, movies, songs, computer software and architecture. Copyright does not protect facts, ideas, systems, or methods of operation, although it may protect the way these things are expressed."* Copyright is designated by the © symbol. Your work is under copyright protection the moment it is created and fixed in tangible form. You do not have to register your copyright to receive protection. However, if you wish to bring a lawsuit for copyright infringement, registration is powerful evidence of authenticity. Registration is easy and inexpensive. You can register on your own or we are happy to assist with the process.

For more information regarding trademarks, visit the United States Patent and Trademark Office website: www.uspto.gov. For information regarding copyright protection and registration, visit the US Copyright Office website: www.copyright.gov.

Get Started!

Now, take the information you discovered in the previous steps and begin to define the personality or character of your company.

What does that character look like? Which qualities stand out? Which areas of promise can you offer and fulfill well? Is the personality of your company innovative, creative, energetic, or sophisticated?

Focus your brand. Narrow it down to a powerful force. This takes thought and can only be accomplished when your objectives for what you want your brand to do for you are clearly understood.

Remember. With your brand, you are reaching for people's hearts and minds, not their wallets. They will not have difficulty buying your material once they have bought in to you. This is the whole point of branding.

Represent Your Brand

Logo Creation

Your logo is the visual symbol of your company or ministry. It is a badge of personal honor, an insignia that instantly and continuously identifies your company. Your logo is a vital piece of your branding process, but it is not the "whole enchilada." People tend to make the mistake of creating a logo before they consider the brand. This results in a logo that does not properly portray the company's best image.

Your logo must be a recognizable symbol that provides consumers with instant and powerful brand recognition. Your products and services are not dependent on your logo for quality or value—your logo is dependent on the quality of your products and services.

Many people consider that their logo is their brand. This is false. As a branding consultant, I advise clients to develop their brand before developing a logo. First establish the strategy of your company and define how your brand will be presented before you attempt to characterize it with a visible symbol.

The notable "swoosh" from Nike® would be no more than a check mark without the strength of the brand. Golden arches would only be yellow rainbows if the hamburgers didn't sell well. The Aflac® duck would be nothing more than a cute cartoon without a careful connection to the corporate message. But all these symbols are instantly recognizable for what they represent because of their connection to their respective brands.

A logo is like a small ad for your company. It is an icon that connects your consumers to your brand. Without the strategy behind it, a logo can easily communicate a wrong message and in return weaken your company's strategy. You need to keep brand recognition consistent with brand message to help increase consumer recognition and trust.

The purpose of a logo is to link the values and goals of your company to a recognizable image.

The purpose of a logo is to link the values and goals of your company to a recognizable image. Make sure that these are clearly established before venturing out to find a logo designer. Be profoundly clear about the message you want your brand to convey. Your logo needs to reflect that message. There must be a strong association between your brand and your logo. Remember, though it is only one piece of your branding strategy, it is an important one.

Your logo should project a sense of professionalism and growth no matter how small your company is. Many logos are not well designed. Often they are created from stock images by a designer who knows nothing more about your company than the name and perhaps a broad industry category.

A visual image is a powerful thing. There is specific psychology behind color choices related to industries. Colors effect how people respond (and which people respond) in a positive way. Designing a logo should not be haphazard or careless. Specific and careful thought should go into the process.

The internet offers a wide variety of graphics that can be used for logo creation. It even offers logo creation sites. These can be helpful and are certainly a low budget option, but such sites are no substitute for a skilled design artist who is also adept at the branding process. The extended specialized background, innovation, insight, and intuition of such a person is worth the investment required to obtain a quality logo. Being professionally branded is worth far more than it costs to contract the process. Hiring a professional is a good option. Hiring the right professional is the very best option you have.

Whether hiring a professional or creating a design on your own, make sure the logo is able to stand up year after year as recognizable, attractive, and identifiable. Consumers must recognize your company by your logo. If it is vague, cluttered, confusing, or misleading, they will miss the point.

Complex logos are generally not strong. Simple is much more powerful. Your logo should capture the eye, be easy to identify, and easy to remember. So, KEEP IT SIMPLE! Think about this easily recognized brand name:

Originally it was "Jerry's Guide to the World Wide Web" but we settled on "Yahoo."

—*Jerry Yang*

The Whole Is Greater

Your brand is dependent on a synergistic relationship between your company and its identity. In this context, synergy is the idea that the whole is greater than the sum of its parts. Nothing could be truer about branding.

Your corporate identity is drawn from all the pieces of the puzzle.

Your corporate identity is drawn from all the pieces of the puzzle, not just a few isolated ideas and visualizations. Core values, core competencies, purpose, mission, and vision need to be expressed in your branding. All communication—written, verbal, audio, or visual must be aligned with your branding strategy. Your logo, your color scheme and design, your print fonts—everything must be consistent. If every piece of literature looks different, people receive a confused message that you do not yet know your own identity. Nobody wants to engage in business with a company that is still trying to "find itself."

Add these together and your brand identity comes to the forefront. Brand identity leads to brand recognition, and brand recognition leads to brand loyalty.

> *Suppliers and especially manufacturers have market power because they have information about a product or a service that the customer does not and cannot have, and* **does not need if he can trust the brand**. *This explains the profitability of brands.*
> — **Peter Drucker**

Conclusion

With your brand developed and your vision becoming marketable, you may find you want to venture into a whole new area—writing a book. The value of a book is enormous, particularly when the book's message is aligned with you, your vision, and your brand.

Writing a book may be the farthest thing from your mind. Or, perhaps you already have the core ingredients of a book but don't know how to put it all together and bring it to print. The next section will explain in detail the process of putting together a book and bringing it to the market. It begins with having something to say, something worthwhile.

Part One Summary

Important points to consider when creating a brand:

◆ Your brand is the imprint of your identity.

◆ Your brand is the foundational piece of your marketing communication.

◆ The branding process begins personally— every company begins with a person.

◆ Your brand is an extension of your name, your reputation. This must be good or the brand is destined to fail. You cannot combat a lack of integrity with a pretty logo.

Below is a list of items to consider when establishing your brand identity:

◆ What products and/or services do you offer?

◆ What is the purpose of your products or usefulness of your services?

◆ What are the core values of your company?

◆ What are your core competencies?

◆ What is the mission of the company?

◆ What does your company specialize in?

◆ Who is your target market?

- Who do your products and services attract?

- What does your brand promise?

- What message does your tagline send to your prospects?

- Where is your "Blue Ocean"?

- What characteristics stand out to others and get the attention of your prospects?

Objectives a good brand will achieve are:

- Your brand will deliver your message clearly.

- Your brand must confirm your credibility.

- Your brand connects your targeted prospects emotionally to your company.

- Your brand motivates the buyer to use your product.

- Your brand solidifies user loyalty.

- Your brand protects your intellectual property through the use of trademarks and service marks.

Your logo is the visual symbol of your company or ministry. A good logo is characterized by the following:

- It must be recognizable—providing instant and powerful brand recognition.

- Logo design should come AFTER the brand has been defined.

Represent Your Brand

◆ Your logo links consumers to your company's values and goals.

◆ A good logo is simple and professional. The design should not be overly complex, have too many parts or colors, and should not be confusing These have a negative effect on your brand.

◆ Your logo should capture the eye, be easy to identify, and easy to remember.

Brand identity takes time to establish and care to manage.

◆ Invest wisely in your branding process.

◆ Remain diligent to keep the established brand pure and strong.

A brand is a living entity—it is enriched or undermined cumulatively over time, the product of a thousand small gestures

—Michael Eisner, CEO Disney

Part Two

Writing Your Book

*Courage is what it takes to stand
up and speak; courage is also what
it takes to sit down and write.*

—**Winston Churchill**

Marketing Your Mind

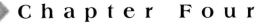

Chapter Four

Something Worthwhile to Say

Paying attention to people's conversation gives you an amazing perspective on human nature. People talk a lot. Even people who think they don't, do. They may hesitate to interrupt when someone else is dominating a conversation, but give a quiet person an opportunity to freely vocalize out of their passion and they will talk.

Everyone has something to say about something. Even people with an impairment or disability communicate using sign language, body language, written words, and visual communications. The trick is getting to that "something" that lights them up and then being willing to listen. Do this a time or two and you might be surprised at what you hear. Even better, you might be amazed at what you learn.

It is not as easy to say everyone is a listener. Hearing is one of the five physical senses we are equipped with. However,

37

hearing and listening are distinctly different. Listening is about mental engagement with thoughts, ideas, and perspectives. Being able to communicate your ideas in an effective way so that others will actually listen and perceive what you are saying is an art. Being able to market your ideas requires that you project your thought processes beyond yourself, leaving an imprint in the minds of others. Whether you are a business person, entrepreneur, minister, or politician, you need to be able to persuade and influence others with your ideas. This too is marketing your mind.

This book is focused on marketing your ideas—your intellectual property. Specifically, it is about creating media from your intellectual property such as books, CDs, DVDs, curricula, profiles, etc. When you write a book, people consider you to be an expert in your field of interest. If you have an area of expertise you feel is beneficial to the lives of others, you must be able to communicate your ideas and experiences in a way that is attractive enough to be purchased.

When you write a book, people consider you to be an expert in your field of interest.

People will only want to listen to your conversation if you have something worthwhile to say. Your message needs to be useful, believable, and functional. When they hear you speak or read your words, you are not actually conversing, but you are communicating nevertheless. You are offering your ideas in an open-ended forum, hoping that someone will take up the conversation in a profitable transaction.

Throughout this chapter, you will need to consider your real situation. Likely, people outside your immediate circle are not particularly interested to engage in your conversation. Most people are not even aware you exist. You have to say something that will pique their interest and cause them to take notice. Your communication has to be loud enough to be heard above the roar of the crowd. It must also be pleasant enough to encourage engagement. If it is obnoxious they will certainly move on. Your communication will have to enter their mind with enough impact to grab their attention and gain an initial hearing. In other words, you must have something worthwhile to say that will cause people to listen rather than just to hear.

People who commit to the process of publishing a book are passionate about their message. They are completely convinced they have something worthwhile to say—something others need to hear. But before you sit down to write your book, you need to consider some very challenging questions. If you are forced to answer any one of them with hesitation, you should carefully revisit your reasons for writing. A book must have a purpose. That purpose may be to inform or to entertain, to encourage or to challenge. Whatever lies at the heart of your motives, your message must be as worthwhile to your readers as it is to you.

Is my Message Credible?

People want to believe. They need to believe. Human nature is wired in such a way that most people are ready to believe what they are told if it is at all credible. This is called *verisimilitude*. It means that something has the appearance of being true or real, even when there is no evidence to support it. When people read a novel or watch a television drama, verisimilitude is a non-negotiable issue. The story and characters must be believable. It must "feel" true.

Verisimilitude has little or nothing to do with honesty or reality. It is based on the perception of truth within a given situation. For instance, when you watch a science-fiction movie, it is often filled with weird and impossible space creatures. The story presents unlikely scenarios that are somehow entirely believable within the context of the film. Things that happen, or characters who appear must be utterly believable in that environment. When they are not, you lose interest quickly and turn away.

Infomercials excel at trying to make the unbelievable believable. They demonstrate products that are, for the most part, things you would not normally purchase. They capture your interest by demonstrating the amazing ability of the product. They enhance the illusion by offering what seems to be greater value—"But wait! If you order now, we'll DOUBLE the offer!" Then in the fine print, they add a shipping and handling charge that in itself would pay for the product. Yet people buy the stuff to the tune of millions of dollars because it seems plausible.

Credibility, on the other hand, is dependent on truth. Facts must be correct. Promises must be sincere. Credibility must be something more than an illusion. The old saying goes, "If it's too good to be true, then it's too good to be true!" Marketers using infomercials and mass media marketing tactics are fishing in a huge Red Ocean. Their expectation is to capture as many fish as possible in a single catch. One customer, one purchase, one piece of the profit pie, and they move on. They know whether or not they are selling junk. They're not interested in building lasting or meaningful relationships. They know people will open their purses for them once and likely never return. If they "catch" a customer and add that together with a million other one-time customers, they have a nice, tidy sum of money in their pockets. Their companies are often shell corporations that can rise and fall with little consequence to a parent company or its reputation.

You, however, are looking to make a difference. You have something to share born from your passion. You have a message that you believe is beneficial to others—maybe even life changing. You are looking to build a long-lasting relationship with people whose lives you will impact in a meaningful way. You are looking to build a brand that will stand, a product that will last, or a service that can be repeated again and again.

Your life must be congruent with your message. You cannot afford to make claims you cannot back up. Your experiences must be real, not inflated or exaggerated. Your

Your life must be congruent with your message.

results must be reproducible in others. Your message must be pure. It must be credible.

Is my Message Useful?

A useful message means you are offering something you know will enhance people's world. When they learn what you know, their efficiency will improve, their character or esteem will be elevated, and their effectiveness will be increased. It is important that you see the usefulness of your message and can quickly and clearly describe that usefulness to others. It is just as important that your readers can recognize how it will benefit them. You must be able to demonstrate that.

What you are offering must be useful based on your clients' needs, wants, expectations, and desires. One of the keys to being successful is to discover a problem, then offer the solution.

Is my Message Practical?

Can someone take what you have to say, practically apply it to their circumstances and see a change? Theories and ideology are only useful if practical application can be made.

Giant ideas need to be broken down into bite-sized chunks. People need specific, measurable goals to successfully advance. When you craft your message, it must be applicable. The person who engages with you should be able to try your ideas and see a result—if not, your message is not practical.

Marketing your mind requires you to translate your ideas into functional reality for those who embrace them. When you craft your message ask yourself, "How can this be applied?" Answer this and you will make your message distinctive and strong.

Is my Message Sensible?

Now there's a word you have to be careful with. To some, sensible means ugly, unstylish, and unattractive. To others, sensible means reasonable, prudent, or well thought-out. For your purposes, prudent and well thought-out are the connotation you seek to advance. In other words, does your idea make sense to the person reading or listening? Do they "get it?" Do they understand the concept? They must believe. Your communication must make sense to them.

If your message doesn't make sense to people, it will not move beyond the advertising stage. You are marketing your mind—your intellectual property. That property must be presented in a way that makes good sense. If a customer finds no sensible reason to purchase what you are selling, they won't.

Even impulse purchases make sense to people at the moment they buy. "I need this." "I want this." "This can help me." "My friend could use this." "This is cool." This is the internal dialogue that precedes a purchase. If a purchase makes sense a transaction is made. Fantastic ideas and life-changing messages are not initially appealing because of their quality. They are appealing because they make sense. That amazing vision you carry in your heart will only be useful if it can be applied. It will only be applied if people buy into it. And people will not buy into it unless it makes sense.

Is my Message Deliverable?

Your idea has no future unless you can convert it into a tangible product or process. You may have a world of aspirations and expectations lined up for your idea. You might have a series of books in your mind or clever inventions drawn on paper. However, if you do not have the capability or the collaboration with others to bring your idea to the marketplace, it will never become a reality. You must be able to deliver your idea tangibly.

> **Your idea has no future unless you can convert it into a tangible product or process.**

A book that is sitting in a dormant file on your computer's hard drive benefits no one. A regimen you have put together to lose weight, improve a marriage, or start a small business helps no one if they can't tap into what you know. You must be able to take your idea across the finish line. Publish the book. Produce the training CD or DVD. Put the curriculum together. Launch the website.

To be deliverable, it must be tangible. Your intellectual property must be packaged in a way that others can access it.

Is my Message Marketable?

Is your idea attractive enough to cause people to respond and purchase it? Marketing your mind is not limited to writing books or putting out informational CDs and DVDs. Marketing your mind might happen as a professional coach or trainer. If you excel at financial planning, health and fitness, personal development, parenting, or some other area of expertise, you can package that know-how in a way that other people can benefit from your knowledge. You can market yourself as a coach or trainer and create collateral training or self-help materials to increase your resource stream.

If you are excited about what you have to offer, other people will join in your excitement. You must consider HOW you will get your message out. How will you package it? How will you produce it? How will people find it? How will they order it? How will it be delivered? To transform an idea into a marketable reality requires that you answer these questions.

It Begins With an Idea

What ideas do you have right now? What consumes your attention? What are most likely to engage others in conversation about? What is your passion? What problem motivates you and drives you to think of solutions? This is where you start. These are clues to discover what you have to say that is worthwhile.

Ideas that you may have abandoned five years ago because they seemed unreasonable may come back in the future. A new marketplace, new market conditions, changing demands and attitudes could radically alter the way people evaluate your idea now. Revisiting a brain storm out of your past may just become a way to see your intellectual property begin to produce a current income stream.

Chapter Five

Write Your Book

A book can be one of your best marketing tools. That's right, a book! A compact, highly informative book in the right hands is an amazing resource. It is more powerful than a business card, more convincing than a brochure, and more personal than an infomercial. It is more durable than a website, more memorable than a billboard, and can be far less expensive than a media advertising campaign.

One of my clients allowed me to assist him in producing a series of three books that educated his potential clients in the process of taking a privately owned company public. In his case, though selling books was a pleasant plus, his true purpose for publishing was to elevate his stature as a successful, respected venture capitalist and land the really big fish. The information in the books is valuable and represents a thorough understanding of raising capital and taking a company public. He delivers this information in layman's terms to educate his clients and help them weigh all their options.

All three books were printed in hard case with foil embossing and beautiful, glossy dust jackets. We wanted to leave the impression with clients that he was the Nordstrom's® option—not Wal-Mart®.

He once told me, "A book is the last business card you'll ever need." It's true. Being an author is special. Even today when

"A book is the last business card you'll ever need."

there is a flood of self-published work on the market, it is still uncommon to meet a published author. Authors are viewed as experts—rare and special, an exclusive group. When you give someone a signed copy of your book, they remember you always. A business card gets tucked in a pocket and is often hidden in a rolodex, forgotten. A signed edition of a book gets kept, particularly if you personalize the inscription. In doing this, you have made the person special, and people remember how you made them feel when they were with you. They will tell others about you and want to be with you again.

Writing a book is a daunting task. Ask a thousand people to write a book and in all likelihood, nine hundred and ninety-nine will refuse out of hand. The other one may try, but with limited success. When people discover I am a publisher, they often tell me they have always wanted to write a book. Unfortunately, few venture past wishful thinking into concrete activity. Why? The task is overwhelming. The process is filled with unknowns and success seems out of reach.

Not long ago we hosted a dinner party at our home. My father, a seasoned author, was in attendance along with my mom and a few of our friends. In passing conversation, it was mentioned that my dad had several books in publication. The comment that followed was quite revealing. One of the guests remarked, "Oh wow, we have a celebrity among us!"

Perhaps the remark was meant to flatter or just to extend the conversation. But such comments reveal a very common perspective. People who have published books are different. They are part of an exclusive club that is far removed from normal people. Authors are special. Authors are experts.

My dad doesn't wear a tweed jacket or smoke a meerschaum pipe. He doesn't cloister himself away for months at a time to find a stream of conscience that will allow him to be creative. Neither do I. We turn our internal dialogue into external expression. We write.

But, I'm not a Writer ...

Objections to writing a book often begin with, "I'm not a writer. I was terrible in English class." It is a fact that some people can communicate on paper better than others. After all, there are very few John Greshams or Max Lucados on the planet. If the truth were known, many of the books you find in Barnes and Noble® were not even written by the person whose name is on the cover. They were written by a professional called a ghost writer. Either that, or the original manuscript was significantly revised by a professional editor. Even so, they authored the idea. The message began in their mind, not the mind of the ghost writer. The book is their story. Yours will be too. And while you will not likely employ a ghost writer, you should gladly be willing to seek out some professional help with your project.

If you are in business, your book will probably communicate some special feature of that business. If you are a minister, your purpose will be to share your revelation and extend the reach of and response to your ministry. In either case, your primary calling and responsibilities are not likely connected to your writing ability.

If you picked up this book, you believe you have an idea worth sharing. Writing a book may be your best option for doing that. The insight you hold is important. Somehow you know it is bigger than you. It should be directed toward others as well. You don't have to be a genius at grammar or a writing wonder—you can still be an author. Just don't try to go it alone. Remember our relay race analogy? You just have to run your leg of the race with focus and excellence. It's okay to pass the baton to others who will help you cross the finish line and meet your goal. Don't let your vision to write a book be erased by the intimidation of the course. That is why I wrote this book. It is my business to assist others through the process of getting their ideas out of their heads and into a marketable format.

> **You don't have to be a genius at grammar or a writing wonder— you can still be an author.**

People come to us at all levels of skill and in various stages of their writing process. In each case, it is our job to minimize the stress and break things down into smaller, reachable goals that follow a commonsense progression. We help them complete the race. We coach them across the finish line.

We help people take the next step and move ahead. Take heart, my friend. It is not as difficult as you think to write and publish a book. It is not necessarily easy, but it is an achievable goal for anyone who is willing to sit down and put their ideas on paper.

The vision must be followed by the venture. It is not enough to stare up the steps — we must step up the stairs.

— Vance Havner

Focus on Your Expertise

Okay, you've finally made the decision to write your book. Hallelujah! So, what are you going to write about? Obviously, you should write about what you know best. Your particular expertise in an area of business or ministry provides you with a world of insight others don't have. Doubtless you have spent a great deal of time in thought, researching and studying the various aspects of your subject matter. You have had conversations over coffee and scribbled notes on a napkin. You know what works and what doesn't. You have discovered through hard experience things you would truly like others to know.

As you begin the writing process, you will soon discover you need a game plan. You should not try to include everything you know about a subject in a single book. If that is your plan, you probably don't know enough about your subject. Either that, or people will need a truck to carry the book you write.

Size is important. Many people will not read a large book regardless of its content. It requires too much commitment to muscle through a 500 page manuscript. If you are writing a history book, a Bible commentary, or a spy novel, huge is acceptable. Business and self-help books that train, equip, and empower people are usually much more succinct and to the point.

Your writing plan should take into consideration the audience you want to reach. Consider their level of education— and I am not referring to their formal education. A college degree in biochemistry will not necessarily equip a person to understand a book about Christian ethics. The educational consideration you are looking at has to do with life experience, practical application, areas of performance, or even areas of dysfunctionality. You want your reader to be able to gain knowledge that will benefit life as they live it. You want to help them discover paths of insight without becoming tangled among the thorns of discouragement along the way.

Every field of endeavor has its own set of parameters. Your book should be developed around one of those. Tell folks how to solve a problem. Show them how to conquer a destructive habit. Teach them a process for success or victory in your area of expertise. Any of these could provide the core ingredients for a truly valuable book. But having the information is only part of the process.

Putting that information into a convincing package requires a systematic, organized approach to your work. Don't be haphazard in your approach. Start with a plan. You need a blueprint for the book you intend to write. This will allow you to include all the necessary components and weed out the stuff that will detract from it.

Start with a plan. You need a blueprint for the book you intend to write.

When you finally do begin to write about your subject, I encourage you to write with raw passion for your topic. Don't get bogged down with too much concern about your grammar, sentence structure, or proper English. If you become wordy or redundant your editor will fix the problem. However, I must stress how important it is to have a purposeful order for what you write.

Following are suggestions with regard to the construction of a book. Please do not use this as a "cookie cutter" formula for writing your book. Your book must be you, not me. These suggestions are meant to be guidelines to help you build your book, much like you would build a home.

Helpful Hints for Construction

1. Outlines

Begin with an outline. An outline will define the concept of the book you want to write. How large will it be? How many chapters should it contain? What parts of the overall story should be written into which chapters? These considerations will define the boundaries of your manuscript and provide you with structure for your narratives.

Give each chapter a working title. These may change as the book takes shape. In time, you may discover that a planned chapter needs to be positioned in another place or eliminated entirely. Still, you need a blueprint, a guide to help keep you on topic as you write.

Chapter titles remind you of the chapter's content. Don't write about begonias in a chapter you have titled "The Joy of Growing Tulips." Write about tulips. If you need a begonia chapter, put one in. Each segment of your book has an appropriate place. These segments will become the various chapters. They should be developed in a way that takes the reader on an effortless journey through your thought processes to a natural conclusion.

Once you have created a general outline for the book you should try to outline your chapters. Make a punch list of the things you need to say in each specific subject area. Keep the list small enough to maintain an attractive chapter size. Make it large enough to cover the subject in an ample, yet succinct way.

With such an outline in hand, you can stay focused on your subject and your initial manuscript will make sense to someone other than yourself.

2. Narratives

A narrative is basically telling a story. Whether fictional or nonfictional, it should be presented in a constructive format. Narratives are a very effective way to communicate an idea or skill set within a book. I encourage their use.

Narratives are especially beneficial in books written to encourage and empower people. Personal reflections of how the application of principles proved to be successful offer hope to the discouraged and give them strength to try. A narrative can be an anecdotal story about another person or other people with similar experiences. Though commonly used in the writing of fiction, narration has become widely popular in spiritual writing as well. Jesus told stories—we call them parables. It worked for Him and it will work for you.

Personal experience is a great communication device. Testimonial evidence, while subjective, is highly useful in gaining a desired response. "If I can do this, anyone can!" It resonates with people. Narratives within the context of a book can be refreshing and they are enjoyable to read. People love stories. The impact of a story often changes a "no" to a "yes," or at least to an "I'll consider it."

When including a narrative in your manuscript, be careful to keep to the salient facts. Narratives tend to wander, touch irrelevant areas, and create confusion in the reader. In a novel, intricate characterizations and long narrative passages create intrigue and interest. In a non-fiction effort, meandering through irrelevant material is distracting and dilutes the focus of your book.

3. Quotations

Another device used in writing is quotation. To quote is to extract a thought, an idea, or a relevant statement from another author and write it into your book. This tool allows you to include other opinions, disarming humor, or succinct commentary in your manuscript. It can also allow you to invoke the authority of a qualified expert.

> *I love quotations because it is a joy to find thoughts*
> *one might have, beautifully expressed with much*
> *authority by someone recognized wiser than oneself.*
> **—Marlene Dietrich, German movie actress (1901 - 1992)**

Using quotations can be problematic, however. Overuse can diminish the strength of your personal knowledge and expertise. Underuse can leave the impression that you have not considered the opinions of others or have no validating support for your views. A well thought-out sprinkling of relevant quotations gives your book a pleasant flavor, like adding herbs to cooking.

A complete set of grammatical rules accompanies the effective and proper use of quotations. What you need to understand for now has to do with using quotations which are germane to your material.

The wisdom of the wise, and the experience
of ages may be preserved by quotation.
–Benjamin Disraeli

Using quotes in a haphazard manner can pad your manuscript, resulting in a needlessly wordy or confusing document. Having endless Scripture quotations, for instance, does not make your book more spiritual. Including extended passages may actually drown out the point you are trying to make. Though it is clear in your mind, you must not assume that others will interpret your conclusions without explanation.

It is better to paraphrase a passage of Scripture or give a specific reference. You should emphasize the meaning you intend to convey and provide a reference to the source. This can be done either directly in the manuscript, or as a footnote or endnote. Again, standard grammatical rules apply.

Including quotations in your manuscript is an interesting and perfectly acceptable way of driving a point home. Adding a pithy comment from some famous (or even infamous) person may not have anything to do with your immediate subject. However, it may shed light on, provoke humor in, or add interest to an otherwise tedious section of your book.

I maintain a file of quotations on a variety of subjects that hold my interest. I find it helpful to refer to a list of pertinent quotations as a part of my preparation when I speak or write. Having these close at hand saves time and provokes thought. You do not need to include every quotation you list. In fact, you shouldn't. Having a "deep well" of useful quotations allows you the option of using something different on the spur of the moment.

4. Research

> *If you steal from one author, it's plagiarism;*
> *if you steal from many it's research.*
> — ***Wilson Mizner***

When writing non-fiction, research is tremendously important. Accuracy when using facts and figures is non-negotiable. Someone who reads your book will know if what you are saying is actually true. Most successful fiction writers also spend considerable time and energy doing research. Either that, or they employ trusted associates to ensure their background information and story lines are accurate. Imagine a Tom Clancy novel without the intricate details of a sustained military operation. The credibility of your work depends on the credibility of your resources. So be accurate.

Unskilled authors are notorious for "shooting from the hip," providing inaccurate details and indefensible conclusions in their work. In the process, the validity of what they actually know and communicate is lost in the clutter of imprecision.

Others fill a book with too much research and not enough of what they want to say that is their own. Research is meant to prove an idea or theory. If you are unclear about what you are trying to say, offering a list of definitions and statistics in hopes the readers will come to some kind of a conclusion is unacceptable.

We don't ask research to do what it was never meant to do, and that is to get an idea.
—William Bernbach

Libraries provide writers with an almost limitless inventory of pertinent information. However, using a library as a resource center can be time consuming and inconvenient. The Internet has provided contemporary authors convenient access to mega-libraries. Research no longer demands countless hours wading through tons of boring facts and details. Even the use of Scripture has found a short-cut by using on-line concordances or Bible software.

A word of caution is needed here. The web has no guarantees. Just because a search engine took you to a site with easy access to data does not mean that the information you acquire is accurate. Using time-honored, well known sources for your information remains a must. Drawing on the commentary from web logs and personal or political websites can be a path to inaccuracy. Always confirm your research with trusted, honest documentation. Always!

One highly respected and sought after minister of the 1980s went through a devastating ordeal as a result of quoting inaccurate information. He actually quoted from a source he assumed he could trust. In so doing, he communicated that a particular author, who had written a self-help book, had committed suicide. The implication that the self-help process had not helped the author made for interesting commentary, but it wasn't true. The author was not dead, and he filed an enormous lawsuit against that minister. So, make sure you have your facts straight.

Now, write!

You have your information in hand. You have your insights in your head. You have the tools at your fingertips. Now, write! Nothing more needs to be said unless and until you begin to commit your thoughts to paper.

Your outline will keep you on point. If you wander, give your editor the freedom to cut material and bring you back to your topic. Your research will provide you with technical details and salient facts. Your list of pertinent quotations will provide you with stimulus when you get stuck or have a mental lapse. So, write!

Most word processing software contains a dictionary, a thesaurus, a spell check feature, and even a grammar checker. Use them. If you get stuck searching for just the right word, but can think of a similar word, the thesaurus will allow you to quickly review a list of alternates. In addition to the tools available in my software, I also keep three specific books in my work area. I recommend you do as well. One is a collegiate dictionary. Another is a thesaurus, because the one connected to my word processor is limited. The third is my college grammar book, because my grammar will never be perfect.

For authors who publish with our company, we provide additional tools to assist them in the writing process. If you visit our website, www.palmtreeproductions.net, you can request a free guide for proper manuscript order, a basic style guide, and a list of common proofreader's marks. These are simple, uncomplicated tools—and are as effective as having a spoon handy when you want to eat soup.

Anything that diminishes barriers to effective collaboration reduces expense, saves time, and strengthens the working relationship. It is helpful for authors, editors, proof readers, and publishers to all work with common grammatical standards. Then the process becomes far less complicated.

The various components in a word processing program are quite good and highly effective. No sincere writer would ever want to be without those innovations. But use caution.

A spell checker does not assess the correct spelling of words which can be spelled in numerous ways. Thus, you must be sure to spell *to*, *too*, or *two* correctly. It is not programmed to spell technical words specific to your field. Fortunately, most word processors have the ability to learn, and you can add new words. Once added, it checks for proper spelling of that word.

Grammar checking software is another story. It cannot be relied on to communicate exactly what you want to say. Grammar checkers do not have the ability to sense the nuance of your words. You will have to treat your grammar checker much like you do your editor. Just say no! If you wrote what you meant, your prerogative as a writer is to leave it where it is. Right or wrong, it's your book.

Grammar software will not argue with you, it will simply leave ugly, squiggly lines under those sentences that do not fit its programmed parameters. Editors may be different. They will fight you, trying to ensure that you use proper English, correct grammar, and reliable punctuation. In most instances, they will be right. You hired them for their expertise and it is usually in your best interest to heed their advice. However, you must be the final judge of the content in your book. Do not let anyone intimidate you into removing or changing your personal communication style. A manuscript may be pristine—perfectly correct in grammar, but sterile. This makes for a boring read. You are unique. Your uniqueness should shine through your writing. Trust yourself. Write what you know. Get going!

The biggest reason people do not write is because they are afraid of criticism:

Afraid to say what they mean,
because they might be criticized for it.

Afraid to be misunderstood, to be accused of saying what they didn't mean, because they might be criticized for it.

Just say it. Say it clearly. Say it now. Say it without fear of being criticized and say it without being boring.

If the goal is no feedback, then say nothing. Don't write.

If the goal is to communicate, then say what you mean.

—Seth Godin

I too had to overcome this fear. Writing a book about writing a book is daring. Advising people on how to construct a manuscript or choose an editor will no doubt invite people to challenge my conclusions and correct my grammar.

I have a friend who wrote a book and received a copy returned to him, completely marked up in red pen. At first, it really shook his confidence. In fact, he was embarrassed. Then he realized that he had already sold over 2,000 copies of that book and received tremendous feedback from people whose lives had been touched and changed through reading it. The one who did the mark up (though offering helpful suggestions) had never published their own work. In the end, it doesn't matter. If you say what you mean to say and someone else is touched by it—who cares about the critics!

Chapter Six

Create Your Biographical Sketch

A Tale of Two Bios

My first English professor in college was unique. She was a bit overweight, had stringy, unkempt hair, and dressed in polyester suits, usually some nondescript shade of beige or taupe. Her pants stopped at least an inch short of her ankles, revealing flat, unstylish, though highly practical shoes. Each day she bustled into class just a few short seconds before the official start time.

Her arms were wrapped around three or four books and a huge stack of paper. Her enormous unzipped purse bulged with more and larger things than it was designed to carry. She also carried a worn briefcase—filled to capacity and beyond.

She entered the classroom each day disheveled and in a rush, but once she settled into "class mode," she magically transformed into an articulate, focused powerhouse of a professor.

Appearances can be deceiving. Hers certainly was. Regardless of her fashion faux pas, I soon developed a healthy respect for her red pen. She established a foundation in the basics of written communication that remains with me to this day.

One day the lesson was about constructing a biographical sketch, often referred to as a "bio." She brought with her two examples. One was quite formal and listed a long pedigree of academic accomplishments, a list of articles published, committees served on, awards received, and proven expertise that distinguished the woman in her field of study. It was impressive—and utterly boring.

The other sketch was of a woman dedicated to her family, including a special needs child. This second woman loved to travel and had been all over the world. She read an average of three novels a week, and volunteered her time for various charitable outreaches focusing on literacy. It told of a love for cooking and a passion for the theatre. The second bio was warm and inviting.

She began the day by allowing us to read both bios. Then she opened the discussion. She asked the class, "Which person would you choose to meet and most like to know?"

Overwhelmingly, we chose the second woman. There was general consensus that she had to be remarkable—like someone you would want to have coffee with or bring along for a road trip. She sounded fascinating.

Next our professor asked which woman we would choose as a tutor, or would ask to mentor us in our career. Unanimously we chose the first woman. She may have sounded dry, but she was obviously well educated, well respected, and completely competent. If she was your tutor, you were sure to succeed.

The professor continued probing us with questions like, "Which woman is friendlier?" and "Which woman is smarter?" In time, the room became divided almost evenly between which woman we would want to have on our team. With a twinkle in her eye, she told us that both women were present in the room. Naturally, we looked around to see who these women might be, because there were no visitors in the room. After a dramatic pause, she revealed to us that both of these biographies were of the same woman—and she was that woman. They were both written about our professor.

The room grew silent as the revelation sank in. My first response was, "no way!" Some students started laughing. Other faces softened as realization that her haphazard appearance was likely due to dealing with her special needs child. Her academic background was certainly more distinguished than our small community college required of its staff. In that hour we became acutely aware that we knew very little at all about our English professor. There was a very full life hidden behind the details. There was much, much more to her than met the eye.

Relevance

The lesson continued with the importance of *relevance* when composing a biographical sketch. You are much more than your bio. Most occasions requiring a bio allow for only a few short sentences or paragraphs in which to frame a person's story. What do you put in? What do you leave out? What matters?

The answer is simple. You put in what is most relevant to the occasion for the biographical sketch. Avoid "fillers" and extra facts—no matter how interesting. If you are speaking at a business conference, your interest in culinary arts, the years you spent as a worship leader, and where you attended high school simply do not matter. These facts may be interesting, but they are not relevant. As you mature and pile up years of experience and achievement, your biographical sketch can easily become cumbersome. Unless you are writing your autobiography, your bio should primarily focus on the pertinent information that qualifies you to present a certain topic to a particular audience.

Credibility

Once you have established which facts are most relevant to your audience, make sure that these facts are credible. If anyone wants to verify the information, the information must be true and valid.

You don't become a "widely sought after international speaker" by speaking to an audience in the Bahamas once upon a time, twenty years ago. Avoid exaggeration. A biography must be honest. There is no reason to "pump yourself up" or speak *"evangel-astically"* about your accomplishments. You are only who you are. You have only done what you have done. You can present yourself to others as great if you choose to. In the end, however, it is God who makes you great, not the image you are trying to project. Honesty and integrity are the strongest possible elements in a biography—pure gold ... everything else is brass (easily tarnished). The apostle Paul says:

> *I'm speaking to you out of deep gratitude for all that God has given me, and especially as I have responsibilities in relation to you. Living then, as every one of you does, in pure grace, it's important that you not misinterpret yourselves as people who are bringing this goodness to God. No, God brings it all to you. The only accurate way to understand ourselves is by what God is and by what He does for us, not by what we are and what we do for Him.[1]*

Tips for Creating a Biographical Sketch

Following is a list of information you should gather and keep handy for creating specific biographical sketches relevant to particular occasions. Remember, you need to have ready access to all the information, but you must use great restraint and include only the most pertinent details as they relate to demonstrating your expertise for the occasion.

1. Create a list of your academic achievements, your accomplishments (including books you have written) leadership positions, organizations and fraternal orders, etc. You may not use all of these, but having a ready access file will allow you to include the appropriate information for a specific bio you must provide.

2. In a single sentence, describe what you are the most passionate about. This creates a thumbnail sketch into your area of expertise.

3. Identify where you live (general, not specific), to whom you are married and for how long, your children and grandchildren (if appropriate).

4. STOP! Consider the purpose of the bio. How will it be used? Is it to introduce you as a speaker at a conference? Is there a conference theme? What is it? What subject(s) are you addressing? What qualifies you to speak on this subject?

   Is your bio for the jacket or back panel of a book? What makes you authoritative on the subject? What qualities do you offer to validate your ability to communicate with others about this?

   Is it for a promotional piece for a seminar, workshop, or self-help video? Similar questions must be applied.

5. Be brief! When people are truly interested in learning more about you, they can and will. So, keep your bio short and focused. They can google you for everything else!

6. Let someone else edit your bio for content. It is difficult to write about yourself. Some people go overboard, listing every possible accomplishment, degree, endorsement, and accolade in their background. Other people are genuinely concerned about appearing to be filled with pride. They will overlook or purposely leave out important information.

   The best advice is to put together your bio then ask your mentor for input and review. Take another pass and determine if you have kept it appropriate to its purpose. Finally, submit it to an editor for any necessary revision or grammatical adjustment.

7. You will likely need several versions of a biographical sketch to provide for different occasions to different audiences. A bio for speaking at a business conference will likely focus on elements that are different from a bio for speaking at a ministry event, and different still for the back of a book or a CD jacket. While all the facts will be true, different facts may be relevant.

8. In some instances, promoters and people engaging you for an event may want a more detailed or personal bio. It is a good idea to have an extended version available that provides a more diverse understanding of your background.

Author's Note:

This chapter opens with a narrative describing a memory from my youth. It is effective in demonstrating my point regarding biographical sketches. This story is taken from a true life experience. However, at the time I didn't take notes and think, "Someday I'll put this in my book." The event is real. The impression my professor made was lasting. Please understand that I took literary license to craft the memory into an enjoyable story for you.

Chapter Seven

The Sprint to the Finish

What comes next? What do you do once you have completed your manuscript? What comes after you transfer what was in your head onto your computer and filed it under "**thebookialwayswantedtowrite.doc**"? There's good news and bad news waiting for you!

The good news is this: you're well on your way to achieving a goal accomplished by only the smallest segment of the population. The bad news is this: you're still a long way from being finished. The real work begins—NOW!

Rewriting What You Wrote

The most difficult part of writing is rewriting. It is easy to fall in love with everything you write. You have put so much of yourself into it. You have labored and toiled and cried and prayed ... It is hard to think of cutting out large portions of material. It is time consuming to rearrange content, or for some chapters to start from scratch!

Let me encourage you. The wonderful thing about rewriting is that you don't have to change everything. Well, sometimes you do—but generally you have to make major changes to only a few things. Here are some suggestions.

1. **Allow some time to lapse between the conclusion of the first draft and the rewrite.** A few days or a week can give you a fresh perspective. Resting time helps you distance yourself from the words and grow more intimate with the story. After all, it's the story that's important.

2. **Before you begin to rewrite, read the entire manuscript.** Mark every passage where you have become redundant or the writing does not seem to flow well. You can come back to these when you finish reading through the whole manuscript. Rework them for better clarity and eliminate needless passages.

3. **Consider your use of adjectives and adverbs.** Descriptive words can be tricky, and the temptation to use auspicious language is huge. Like just now I couldn't resist using the word "auspicious." Writing seems like it should be intellectual, and the use of big words feels intelligent. In spite of my use of the word *verisimilitude* in an earlier chapter, I caution you to use big words sparingly. Use them only when a simpler word fails to convey your meaning. Big words can be so off-putting that people will begin to lose interest in what you are saying. No one wants to read your book with a dictionary opened beside

them. In fact, the use of big words can be and often is taken as an insult.

When you find it necessary to use unfamiliar words or technical terms, be sure to define them. People who know them will not be offended. People who don't will appreciate the fact you cared enough to share what you meant. When people misinterpret the meaning of the words you use, your intent is lost.

4. **Consider the length and complexity of your sentences.** Complex sentences are perfectly acceptable. However, they should not be the standard for your writing. Use simple sentences whenever you can. I have read manuscripts which contained individual sentences of sixty or seventy words. Ugh! Hard to read. Hard to understand.

5. **Consider the length of paragraphs.** Some writers compose extended paragraphs, full of conflicting ideas and lines of thoughts. Short succinct paragraphs are easy to follow. A single sentence can be a paragraph, but it is unusual, used only to emphasize a strong point or make a statement.

A paragraph should be confined to a single thought or specific point. Should that point diverge into two directions, starting a new paragraph is probably a good idea. This has more to do with clarity than with grammatical correctness. There is no hard and fast rule. Your own sense of clarity and communication of your message will dictate how much you write into a single paragraph.

6. **As much as you are able, use proper grammar.** We live in a time when English speaking people have lost much of the precision in their speech. Street language may be acceptable on the street or in a movie script. It is not acceptable in a book unless it is a direct quotation. Your editor will do everything possible to correct your grammatical errors. However, when she does, she may not grasp the intent you meant to convey. If you initially write it correctly, she will not feel the need to adjust it.

It is beneficial to have a grammar guide close by to which you can refer. If you have a question about how a particular sentence should be written or a specific word used, you can easily refer to that guide for help. There are even free online resources to quickly check a rule concerning commas or capitalization. Use them.

7. **Use the correct punctuation.** The most common problem found in written material is the improper use of punctuation. The wrong placement of commas, periods, apostrophes, colons, and semi-colons can confuse the meaning. It also detracts from the authoritative quality of your book. Continuous use of improper punctuation leaves an impression that the author is not an expert after all. Thankfully, your grammar guide contains detailed information about punctuation and your copy editor should be well versed. Shamelessly use them both.

Spend a little time and energy studying grammar and punctuation. No matter your field or occupation, becoming a better communicator is in your best interest. As you write more and more, you will become familiar with what works and what doesn't. You may never be completely satisfied with your grammar. That's okay. A good editor can help a great deal here, but you need to write as accurately and concisely as possible.

8. **Rewrite again.** That's right. Go back over the rewrite for a re-rewrite. If necessary, do this over and over until you get it right. Make your manuscript say what it needs to say. Don't be too easily satisfied. This is your vision, your dream, your intellectual property. It is your mind that you are going to market. Don't weaken your case or sell yourself short by allowing your written material to be substandard. You do not have to be a professional to write well. You simply have to write well. Rewriting is the only way to make that happen.

9. **Stop tweaking.** I have worked with clients who are still tweaking their manuscript a year after it was submitted. Fear of sounding foolish or having your work criticized can keep you from going to print. At some point you must call it quits and go to press. Here is some excellent advice from Seth Godin:

> *Of course it's not done. It's never done.*
>
> *That's not the right question.*

The question is: when is it good enough?

Good enough, for those who seek perfection, is what we call it when it's sufficient to surpass the standards we've set. Anything beyond good enough is called stalling and a waste of time.

The Journey From the Computer to the Publisher

When at last you have a manuscript in hand that you are comfortable with and proud of, it is time to have it formatted for print. It reveals your thought processes and expresses them in clear, concise language. The steps from here on, while perhaps more specific, are generally less demanding on you. That does not mean you can turn loose of your project. It's yours, and you must follow it step by step to turn your intellectual property into a quality, marketable resource.

What steps remain? Can you accomplish it on your own? Yes. You can.

Self-publishing is a viable option and many people choose this route. If you are willing to invest the time to learn what you need to know you can self-publish successfully. Unfortunately, many self-published works have a substandard presentation. No matter how great the content, if the cover design is lackluster and the formatting unremarkable, the end product will fail to reflect the passion and purpose of the message. I have been handed many books from apologetic authors, "Well, I published it myself. Someday I'd like to have it done professionally."

I have also experienced the opposite end of the spectrum. I have been handed a book that was absolutely terrible—in every way! Yet, the author was practically beaming when he handed me his "baby." He was totally convinced he had the next New York Times best seller undiscovered in his hand. I didn't have the heart to tell him I saw four spelling errors on the back jacket without even looking closely. The graphic design was a mid-level effort at best and fell far short of real professionalism. Please ... don't get me started!

Help is available. Help is affordable. Do you cut your own hair? Tailor your own suits? If so, I recommend you self-publish. If you recognize that sometimes the touch of a professional is worth the effort, then you may consider other alternatives.

There are many publishing houses out there. Most have a "vanity publishing" arm. This means they will publish your work no matter its content. As long as they get paid for their services, they'll get you in print. To be picked up by a publishing house that pays YOU for your manuscript is quite rare ... and wonderful. This happened for one of our clients for whom we have done extensive branding work and have assisted publishing several works. He put in the effort to market his mind, establish his brand, and get his message out into the mainstream. He has been rewarded with a contract from a national publisher. How exciting!

The final chapter of this book is the Palm Tree Productions story. It will give you some insight about why we got into this business in the first place. It also explains why we feel so strongly about helping authors get their work in print in a way they can be proud of. We aren't the right fit for everyone, and we don't try to be. We're good at what we do and we love doing it for the people who fall into our niche market.

Steps to Publishing

1. The Editing Process

Whether you self-publish or decide to seek assistance with publishing, getting your work into the hands of an editor is an absolute must. Having spent many hours focusing on your work, the tendency to overlook errors increases. True, editing your own work will be less expensive. Presenting a book filled with grammatical, punctuation, and descriptive errors usually proves to be costly in other ways. This is one step you should not skip.

Editors are trained to specifically discover weaknesses and identify areas where there is a lack of continuity in your manuscript. They look at the construction of your sentences, punctuation, the use of descriptive words, and a host of other specific areas. In the end, they will deliver your manuscript, covered with proofreader's marks and helpful suggestions. These criticisms are meant to help you uncover the areas you overlooked, not disparage or demean your efforts.

Take care when you employ an editor. Some editors are so rigid in their approach that the finished product no longer sounds like you. All elements of personal style are removed in order to conform to a set style sheet. Always send an editor a sample of your work and review how they handle that. Agree to work with them only if the sample experience goes well.

Can you communicate well with each other? Did they improve your work without stripping it of your style? Can you work with them for a long process? These are important questions to be answered. No matter how many editors you employ, they will each find different things and disagree about the application of writing rules. It is best to find one you like and can trust, then stick with them. Just like "too many cooks spoil the broth," too many editors ruin a story.

2. The Order of Your Manuscript

How you lay out your manuscript is important. Books are published with slight variations in this layout, but most contain the same basic information. On the following page is the manuscript order we recommend to our authors. Laying out your manuscript in this fashion makes the formatting process easier for us and less expensive for you. Remember, it is not necessary to contain all the elements listed. This is just the usual and customary order in which they appear should you choose to use them.

Suggested Manuscript Order

◆ **Title Page**—Sometimes a "Half Title" precedes this.

◆ **Copyright Page**—Always located on the back of the title page.

◆ **Dedication**

◆ **Table of Contents**

◆ **Foreword**—The foreword is written by someone other than the author, an expert in the topic or field if possible. A foreword by a well known or respected individual lends credibility to your work.

◆ **Preface**—The preface is written by the author, it is the story of how the book came into being: genesis and purpose.

◆ **Acknowledgements**—This section is made up of expressions of gratitude, indebtedness for contribution, etc.

NOTE: The pages listed above are numbered with lower case Roman Numerals.

◆ **Introduction**—This is also written by the author and deals with the subject of the book, supplementing and introducing the concept or indicating a point of view to be adopted by the reader

◆ **Chapters**

◆ **Appendix**—This would include any closing materials such as a study guide, end notes, glossary, about the author, etc.

Note: *Endorsements are encouraged and often appear on the back jacket of the book. Should you have extended endorsements that you want to include within the manuscript, these may appear after the dedication or as final pages.*

3. ISBN and LCCN

If you intend to have your book sold in a bookstore or through a venue such as amazon.com, you will need an ISBN (International Standard Book Number) and the corresponding bar code. The price of your book can also be included in the bar code if you desire. The ISBN bar code will appear on the back jacket and the 13-digit number should also appear on your copyright page.

It is important that you obtain a number from a reputable source that will properly enter your book's data into the national database registry where all ISBN's are catalogued. I have a friend who purchased a cheap ISBN online and had it printed on her book only to discover later that it belonged to a book already in print. Her number was not valid and her book could not be sold in bookstores.

You may also desire to obtain a Library of Congress Control Number (LCCN). This is a requirement only if your book is going to be offered in academic libraries. This number also appears on your copyright page and only becomes valid when the registration process is complete and an actual printed book is filed with the Library of Congress in Washington, D.C.

4. **Cover Design and Formatting**

Before you can go to print, your book will need to be formatted. It will also need a cover or jacket. Creative, innovative design makes your book appealing and highly marketable. Formatting either enhances or detracts from your message. Visual appeal is a key selling feature. The cover needs to grab attention and make someone want to pick your book up to find out what's inside. Beautiful formatting—font selection, print size, width of margins, specialized text, illustrations, etc. are all considerations that must be taken into account.

5. Copyright Protection

The protection of your copyright is also extremely important. In fact, this is the area that sets us apart from most others in the business. Our authors maintain their copyright and all privileges. They own the work completely. They can choose to print with us or through any source that best suits them. They are given print-ready files and have the freedom to create as many copies as they like. Not having control of your own copyright means you no longer control your intellectual property. *(Basic copyright protection was introduced on page 23.)*

Many publishing houses restrict authors from printing with anyone other than the publisher. They require authors to purchase their own books from them at wholesale prices before they can sell them at retail to customers. Most vanity publishing agreements also have "buy-back" clauses. These require authors to purchase all unsold copies from the publisher after a specified length of time. Be sure to read the fine print of any agreement and make sure your interests are well protected.

You may want the help of a professional, but not want their publishing house information to appear on or in your book. Make sure this is a viable option if it is important to you. Palm Tree offers "blind publishing" to meet this need. Some authors wish to have their books published under their own business or ministry name and we gladly help with this endeavor. Most of those we serve appreciate the quality of their experience with us and proudly bear the Palm Tree Productions logo on the back of their book.

6. Proofreading

Proofreading is not the same thing as editing. Proofreading is the final stage of typographic production before going to press. Proofreading ensures that words are spelled correctly, no doubled words are included (that that), and sentences end with proper punctuation. Proofreaders also check formatting to make certain that the style of layout is consistent throughout each chapter.

Every word in a book should be proofed. This includes title pages, copyright information, headers, footers, footnotes, pull-quotes (those interest grabbing segments printed in the margins), cover text, biographical sketches, and advertisement pages when included. Nothing escapes the scrutiny of a proofreader. When the book goes to press, it is important to have errors corrected. This makes for a very professional outcome and makes you look good. Remember, however, proof readers are human. Even New York Times best sellers have the occasional typographical error. Few books are perfect, but every effort should be made to present a "clean" manuscript.

7. Printing your Book

There is a lot of room for error when choosing a printer. Some presses will not even work with an individual author—the learning process is just too involved and they don't have time to educate you. There are more accessible print-on-demand options for a self-published author, but these can be expensive per book. If you plan to print on your own, be prepared to do some research. It is important to have good quality paper, straight trimming, good binding, the right coating ... and so many other things! It is my recommendation to seek help with the printing process. In most cases, your result will be comparable in price, but so much better in process and product.

8. Inspecting the Final Product

When your books arrive from the press, be sure to physically inspect the boxes for any appearance of damage. I recommend you open several of the cases and make sure that the entire run is of consistent quality. The time to make a damage claim against a shipping company or request a reprint from a press is usually 30 days or less. If you open a damaged box six months after it has arrived, you're out of luck. Make sure all is well before you sign off on that shipment.

Part Two Summary

Writing begins with having something worthwhile to say. There must be a purpose and a passion motivating the manuscript. Following are the questions we addressed to determine the strength of a message:

◆ Is the message credible?

◆ Is the message useful?

◆ Is the message practical?

◆ Is the message sensible?

◆ Is the message deliverable?

◆ Is the message marketable?

When it is determined that an idea has enough merit to commit to a manuscript, it is time to write:

◆ You do not have to be an accomplished writer or grammarian to author a book. This limitation can be overcome by allowing others to help you construct or edit your material once you have put the initial thoughts on paper.

◆ Focus on your expertise. Your strongest material will come from what you are the most passionate about and have the most experience behind.

- Begin with a plan. I discussed the use of outlines, narratives, quotations, and research to help with the construction of your manuscript.

- Use the tools that are available to you. I encouraged the use of spell checking and grammar checking software. I also recommend keeping a collegiate dictionary, thesaurus, and basic grammar book handy when writing. Finally, I offered additional author tools available for free when you visit our website: www.palmtreeproductions.net. These are a manuscript order, a basic style guide, and common proofreader's marks.

- Finally, I addressed the most frequent obstacle to writing a book that I have encountered— fear of criticism. Putting your ideas on paper is concrete. You can't back away from them. When you establish yourself as an expert in your field, expect criticism. When you overcome this fear and trust yourself—trust the message that God has placed inside of you—you are ready to write!

Tips for creating your biographical sketch:

- Always consider the relevance of the details you are including to the occassion for the bio.

- Make sure the presentation of your facts is credible and verifiable.

- Specific items to consider when creating a bio are addressed on pages 70-71.

The sprint to the finish is what comes after you have completed the rough draft of your manuscript. I addressed the following:

- Helpful suggestions to consider during the process of a rewrite (found on pages 74 - 77).

- Steps to publishing—getting your book in print—were discussed as well. These were:

   - The Editing Process

   - Manuscript Order

   - ISBN and LCCN

   - Cover Design and Formatting

   - Copyright Protection

   - Proofreading

   - Printing Your Book

   - Inspecting the Final Product

When you speak, your words echo across the room.
When you write, your words echo across the ages.

— Bud Gardner, author of Chicken Soup for the Writer's Soul

Part Three

Marketing Your Media

Marketing is not an event, but a process ...
It has a beginning, a middle, but never
an end, for it is a process. You improve
it, perfect it, change it, even pause it.
But you never stop it completely."

—Jay Conrad Levinson

Chapter Eight

Reaching
People

Everything you do is marketing—your life must be congruent
with the brand you establish or it will never get off the ground.

—Wendy K. Walters

A fter branding yourself and creating a tangible product, you are at long last ready to market your intellectual property. It is no longer just a dream. You have accomplished a remarkable feat. Now you have to take it to another level. It is time to sell what you have created. You have to sell your material. More specifically, you have to sell yourself. That can prove to be a challenge.

Some people never seem to develop the confidence necessary to promote themselves. Others are so shameless in self-promotion it is nauseating. Remember this: any skill can be learned by a reasonably intelligent, properly motivated individual. You can do this if you want to. Why wouldn't you? You've taken the first steps. You've matured into a well-branded, highly marketable individual (business or ministry) ready to release your intellectual property to a waiting clientele. What you have is important. What you have is valuable. What you have is the culmination of years of study, effort, and experience. No one—absolutely no one, can bring what you bring to the marketplace. You are unique. That is what finally will make you successful.

Tell Others What You Have to Offer

For people to buy into your product or service, you must be able to point to what you have successfully accomplished, demonstrate what you are achieving now, and communicate your plans for the future..

—Wendy K. Walters

Nothing gets sold unless someone knows it is for sale. There are many ways to tell people what you have to offer. A national television campaign will reach a lot of people, but it will cost a fortune to accomplish. A website or YouTube® posting will be relatively inexpensive by comparison, but may or may not reach your targeted audience.

Nothing gets sold unless someone knows it is for sale.

You must tell people what you have to offer. You must offer what people want to meet a specific need or fulfill a desire in the context of their lives.

Your market will depend largely on your product or idea. Small focused markets are called niche markets, and they can be quite profitable. However, your means of reaching them must be creative. We will cover many ideas in this section to help you.

Your ideas will have to be presented in ways that produce a response, preferably an emotional one—*I want it!* It must be a practical one as well—*I can use it, I need it, it will be beneficial to my work, my play, or my future.*

Telling them Where and How They Can Get It

The next thing people need to know is where your product can be obtained. They need to know how they can purchase your material or schedule an event. Availability is the key to moving your material.

Availability is the key to moving your material.

Many of our clients have a ready-made platform from which to sell. They own their own business, pastor a church, or provide inspirational or motivational speaking. This allows them to sell products through conferences or through their own businesses. Many have also been successful getting their product into privately owned bookstores, coffee shops, and gift boutiques. Other outlets such as amazon.com and barnesandnoble.com are also a way to get your product into the market.

Beyond that, a website is an absolute must. It doesn't matter if your company is one person, five people, or five hundred people strong—a website can help level the playing field. I will expand this concept as we go along.

Tell Them Why They Need to Buy From You

Once you have moved past the obstacles of getting your material into a marketable package, you still have another hurdle to cross. People need to know why buying from you is better than buying something similar from someone else.

There are several reasons your idea is best. First, it's yours! True, it is possible someone else has the same or similar ideas, but they have not processed them like you have. You need to confidently believe and clearly communicate that yours is a better solution. Literally thousands of self-help books clutter the literary landscape. If you are going to produce a self-help package—books, videos, CDs, etc., you will need to have an approach that is different from others in that field. For example, the huge number of physical training and weight loss programs available is astounding. They could not all possibly work—if they did you would see far more skinny people roaming the streets. The fact that old ideas continue to sell while new ideas flood the market is proof that there is room at the table for your idea.

Your job is to communicate the superiority of your product, service, or information without compromising your integrity, manipulating your customer, or losing sight of the true value of your product. Not everyone needs what you have to offer.

Please do not try to push it on them. When you remain true to yourself and your calling, you are able to look in the mirror, know that you have successfully translated your ideas into profitable material, and offered them at a fair, competitive, and reasonable price. People will appreciate your integrity and your product or service will be accompanied with an ever-increasing approval on the part of your consumers.

Give Back

I would be remiss if I didn't encourage you to have a plan for your profits. As surely as you need a plan to market, you need a plan to give. I sincerely want to encourage your generosity of spirit. It is congruent with my own values, and has proven to be a valuable asset in my life.

Most of the people who contract our services have a larger mission or vision which they are trying to support. Their purpose for marketing their intellectual property extends beyond making the message available. It also helps to generate an income stream which they can use to support their mission. I am deeply convicted that profits should have a purpose. I firmly believe that planned generosity should be at the core of every marketing strategy. Most of the successful people I know exhibit this quality in every area of their life—including their business.

The generous will prosper; those who refresh others will themselves be refreshed.[1]

Marketing Your Mind

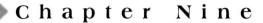

Chapter Nine

Identifying Your Niche

I have met many people who believed they had something worthwhile to say and believed it was worthy of a broad audience, but they were convinced only those who get a "big break" or are "discovered" get the chance to make an impact. Okay, so you're not John Maxwell, Zig Ziglar, or Suze Orman. You are you. You may or may not be ready to reach the entire nation with your innovative ideas. You are, however, capable of expressing yourself with excellence and finding your place in the market.

How do you locate your niche? How do you discover where your particular brand and message are wanted, needed, and will make a difference? I have two suggestions. Listen to yourself, and listen to others.

Listening to yourself will take some practice. Most of our thoughts have to do with everyday matters. *What should I wear? What do I want to eat? Did I turn off the coffee pot?* To some degree, you need to tune those out. The thoughts you need to tune in are connected to your passion, your expectations, your desires—even your disappointments. Too little time is given just to think, to ponder those things that are important. The ambient noise in our twenty-first century lives drowns out meaningful thoughts that can help us grow, in favor of the fleeting, trivial thoughts that require little focus, effort, or concentration.

What would my life be like if ...? What would I do if I were given the opportunity to ... ? When you ask these kinds of questions you begin to expose your niche market. Your areas of interest and expertise are not isolated. They represent a segment of people who carry similar interests and feelings. That's the point. You know things they don't know. You have experiences and knowledge that would be helpful to them. Perhaps that's a niche where you can fit your program into their world. If you can, you have a ready-made market for your intellectual property.

You have more available to you than your own musings, however. You have other people's thought processes as well. They, like you, process millions of thoughts every day. They have to decide what to wear and what to eat just like you do. They also have needs and desires they wish someone would meet. *"If someone would just come up with a way for me to ..."* ... and there it is. You do! You have a way. It's in your package. It's written in your book. It is presented on your CD. Your video is produced and waiting for distribution. All you have to do is connect your published information with their unmet need. That's a niche.

Find the "Blue Ocean"— What Makes You Special

Earlier, we talked about "Blue Ocean" vs. "Red Ocean" marketing. It is almost impossible to find a niche in the Red Ocean. There are just too many fishermen angling for the same fish. Someday, if the circumstances all come together, you may tap into that market. I truly hope you do. Until then, however, a niche market is your best option to find profitability for your intellectual property. You need to discover your Blue Ocean.

What makes you special? What causes you to stand out from the crowd? What is it about your message, your training perspective, or your specialized knowledge that could possibly give you an edge? That is where the Blue Ocean begins. You need to capitalize on that aspect of your message and push that to the forefront of your efforts to market your mind.

You may find the thing that sets you apart is not what you are most interested in doing. You could ignore your Blue Ocean opportunity and choose instead to slug it out with the competition. Or, you could find a way to use this unique part of your message to reach an untapped audience. In the process, you will be able to communicate those things which are closest to your heart and mind.

Blue Ocean for intellectual property is not so much about your specific message as it is finding a way to deliver your message with appeal. Your message will not reach anyone until it reaches someone. Your ability to communicate, the excellence of your writing, and the power in your presentation will cause people to see the importance of what you are telling them. But first, they have to give you the opportunity to tell them. Pay attention to what others indicate they want to hear. Find out what they want to know. This is one of the ways to discover your niche and secure your place in the market.

Which Marketing Tools Should You Use?

Being able to describe or define marketing in an uncomplicated, straightforward manner would be a wonderful thing to do. It is not possible. Marketing has too many twists and turns to be nailed down into a precise, unchanging format. You will need to be flexible, innovative, and determined if you are to be successful. The next two chapters will unveil several effective marketing perspectives. The first group offers people strategies that are effective for marketing a service, developing speaking opportunities, or presenting some type of class, program, or seminar. The second directs you to Internet strategies. That medium is more practical to market a product you have created—books, CDs, DVDs, workbooks, etc.

It is important for you to use several strategies, not just one or two. You can benefit from each of these marketing tools in your inventory. While one or two of them may prove to be better for your particular application, all of them are effective and should be pursued.

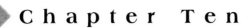
Connecting With People

In this chapter we will look at three strategies—relationship marketing, endorsements, and referrals. They are all dependent on connecting directly with people. While they can be used with other marketing strategies, each has the element of being closely involved with verbal communications. Because of that, they are well suited to communicating the value of your service, the effectiveness of your message, or the usefulness of your program. They also have strength in communicating the worth of the product you have produced as intellectual property, so don't sell them short.

Relationship Marketing

Relationship marketing is perhaps the most valuable strategy. Not only is it good for your business, it has intrinsic rewards that far outweigh a potential business transaction. People matter.

I believe the first rule of relationship marketing is to be authentic. If you are confident in who you are and what you are called to do, you never have to shrink back or puff up. Just fill the space God gives you. If you are flexible enough to expand and contract with the changing opportunities and seasons, you'll be just fine.

The first rule of relationship marketing is to be authentic.

Building new relationships is not always an easy task. However, people who have heard of you or your services may well desire to know you as an individual before they are willing to do business with you. If you are breaking into the consulting or coaching arena, they need to trust you and like you before they want to work with you. A telephone call or Skype chat can be a wise investment. If you have the opportunity to meet in person, that is even better. Not only will the potential client find out if the chemistry is right, you too will have the opportunity to engage or pass. If your market is larger than one-on-one will allow, posting videos on your website or YouTube can be very effective. It gives people a sample of your communication style, your rhythm, your sense of humor, and your passion. Like it or not, you live in a video generation. If you want to market your ideas, you are going to have to engage in a way that people can connect to visually. It helps them connect emotionally.

If you have a circle of relationships, being endorsed by others in that circle is a powerful tool. People who have used your services and are pleased tend to tell their friends and acquaintances about you. Folks genuinely want those around them to succeed. If they find a special sale or had an amazing dining experience they will almost always communicate that. If they discover a company that provides really good service, they will communicate that as well.

Most people have more than one circle of friends. Most have several different circles of friends or associates. You may be in one of those circles but not in another. Those are closed loops—not especially open to outsiders except by invitation. To be invited in as an expert or service provider requires endorsement by someone already inside that circle. Once inside, the possibility of working with other individuals inside that circle grows strong. They too have circles beyond the one you just entered. In time, you could find your business expanding quite well because you invested in cultivating those relationships. Relationship marketing is often the very best marketing strategy—especially in a closed loop, or niche.

At conferences and events, I have experienced getting to know someone and developing that relationship for a year or longer before any business was ever initiated. I am more interested in capturing their heart and their mind. If we do business later, relationship has already been established and moving forward with business has a firm foundation from which to build. This isn't always practical. As your business grows, demands for your time and energy will require you to establish boundaries in this area. But whenever you have an opportunity to network with others—whether attending an event or as the keynote speaker—few things are a bigger turn-off than encountering someone who is too important to take the time for a friendly conversation.

Referrals

I received an email from a friend with the following statement: *"A referral is the ultimate compliment. It is sending someone you care about to someone you trust."* I have no idea if this was original or borrowed, but I love it! A referral is larger than an endorsement. The stakes are higher. It goes beyond sharing a good experience and now personally vouches for the one providing that experience.

> *Always do the right thing and give your best. If you treat people well they will gladly refer others to you.*
>
> ***Wendy K. Walters***

People care about what other people think and say. For everything from booking a hotel room to choosing a plumber, we tend to check out customer reviews. Even though the reviews may be made by total strangers, we tend to value the objective opinion of others enough to consider what they have to say before making a buying decision. If three people said the hotel was noisy and the staff was unfriendly, this matters. If three people said the plumber was professional, cleaned up after himself, and gave a good price, you're probably going to call the guy. Now, that is how much we value the opinion of strangers. How much more when the door is opened by someone we are already in relationship with? If someone you know and trust recommends a product, person, or service, your opinion will be positive and receptive from the beginning. Word of mouth works—for you or against you.

Another powerful marketing tool is to offer a finder's fee or percentage of a sale as a thank you for a referral that turns into paid business. This further motivates people to recommend your product or service. It is a nice way to reward others for loyalty.

When possible, connect your clients to each other. You will eventually discover that one of your clients has an area of expertise needed by another one of your clients. Refer them to each other. Connect them. Spread the love. Share the goodwill. Pay it forward. This is the Golden Rule in action. I remember it when someone refers someone to me. It is a tribute to my passion to provide for the success of others, and I highly value the confident expectation that I will deliver on this promise.

Endorsement Marketing

The Bible offers some wise counsel concerning marketing:

Let another praise you, and not your own mouth;
someone else, and not your own lips.[1]

The balance between blowing your own horn and letting someone else play your song is delicate. It should not be ignored.

Being endorsed by someone else is validation of the integrity and authenticity of your presentation. An endorsement is what a person says or writes about you (your product, or your service) in a favorable manner and recommends that others buy it based on their experience. In essence they ask you to take their word for it. An endorsement communicates to others that your brand is an honest brand, and that what you promise will actually be fulfilled. People will be thrilled to know you are who you say you are, and they will take delight in working with you. When they have a positive experience, they too will endorse you among their friends and colleagues.

It is okay to ask for an endorsement. If you speak at a conference or seminar, it is entirely appropriate to ask the host for a short testimonial of their experience with you. If you complete a team project, it is fine to ask your colleagues for a review of your contribution. If you have written a book, it is usually considered an honor to ask someone you have a relationship with to review and endorse it.

When asking for an endorsement, be careful not to overreach yourself. If you do NOT have a relationship developed, you must exercise extreme caution. That doesn't mean you can't ask, but you must ask with humility and not get ruffled if the answer is no, or there is no answer at all. Celebrities and well-known personalities get asked often to endorse things they have no knowledge of or experience with. I would advise great restraint. Use your best contacts and most viable sources, but maintain your integrity—and your dignity.

It is also acceptable to seek customer testimonials for use in marketing. Many people are delighted that you care about their opinion and are happy to share their experience. You can send out a short survey, leave a place on your website for customers to post comments, or simply ask them outright. Happy customers attract more customers.

We expect a company to tell us the good stuff, but when a happy customer or trusted expert sings your praises without self-interest, it is more believable. It has greater weight. This is more effective than the professionally developed marketing language presented by the company faithful. Carefully crafted language is an absolute must, but the power of endorsement should not be overlooked.

Make the Connection Personal

Once you do receive an initial call from a prospective client and they seem interested in going to the next level, take the initiative. Schedule a follow up call at a time convenient for them. Whenever possible, schedule a face to face meeting. Most of our clients are not local, but whenever reasonable we make ourselves available to them, either when they travel into our area or we travel into theirs. The personal touch is still the most powerful touch. A visit is better than a phone call and a phone call is better than an email. Show genuine interest in people and they will reward you with loyalty to your product and your brand. Abuse them and they will disappear.

The personal touch is still the most powerful touch.

Connecting with a client is more about learning who they are than demonstrating to them who you are. Learn all you can about them. Ask questions and listen attentively to their answers. People know if you are answering someone else's email while you are on the telephone with them. Be present in the conversation. Give them your undivided attention.

Have detailed knowledge of pricing and options. When you can break it down to the bottom line, you are halfway there. They may love you ... but are you in the ballpark? To have a meeting with a prospective client without someone breaching the subject of cost is unusual. Being able to answer questions honestly and without hesitation is critical. Fumbling around for an answer, or weakness in your voice can reverse a decision they have made. Be confident in what you offer and do not apologize for the price. If you're the right fit for them, price will not be a barrier. If you are the wrong fit, you will both be unhappy in the end.

Lastly, have your branded material available. Present it to the client. This can be done through your website, by email or snail mail, and when at all possible, in person. This brochure, flyer, or press kit will become a reminder to them after your initial connection has passed. Be prepared to give references and present examples of your work. This is important in establishing your connection to your client as a trusted expert or provider.

Chapter Eleven

Marketing to the Masses

How do you reach people with your message when you do not know them and will never meet them? Marketing strategies to reach the masses are varied. We will look at three of the most accessible strategies and you will have to determine whether or not you will invest the time, finances, and energy necessary to utilize them.

Website

The Internet has changed marketing forever. Every company, regardless of its size, now has the potential of going global. Because of the Internet you can market your intellectual property to an international audience. You are not limited to your home town, your local radio station, or your newspaper's subscription base.

Every company, regardless of size, should have its own website. Yours may be a "one man show" with you as chief cook and bottle washer. Your website won't show that unless

Every company, regardless of size, should have its own website.

you put the information in there. What it will show is your brand. The offering of your intellectual property will not depend on a fancy corporate office, a specialized facility, a huge warehouse, or dedicated logistics. The offering of your intellectual property must clearly demonstrate excellence and expertise. Nothing compares to the effectiveness a website has to achieve this objective. Your website is simply an electronic presentation of anything and everything you would like people to know about you and your business.

Your website address should appear on every piece of information and media you publish. Even if your location or phone number changes, it is easy to keep your website updated with the current contact information.

You must have a website. It will help if it is both attractive and informative. It doesn't need to be flashy or have fifty subpages. It does need to be visually appealing, informative, and easy to navigate. As you grow, your website can grow with you.

Checking out a website has become a first response when someone wants to learn about you. My children don't even know what a phone book looks like. Smart phones and other hand-held devices make the Internet accessible and convenient. What does your website present? How is your image made strong by what they see and read? These are important questions.

People will also use the web to research the integrity and viability of your business. In our media-driven culture, people tend to express their dissatisfaction in writing and display it for all to see on the Internet. Do everything you can to maintain your integrity and credibility in your Internet presence.

Web developers offer a wide variety of development options to individuals and businesses. The more complex your website, the more it will cost to have it created. Of course, you can design and populate your own website with information. There are many "template driven" options available that are affordable and cover the basics. Having a simple, well designed site is better than having an elaborate mess.

An effective website for marketing should be easy to navigate with a clear "About Us" and "Contact" page. If you are selling products, you need a simple "Store" with "click and shop" capability that is easy to use with clean graphics and logical process to purchase easily. I recommend a page for "Endorsements" or "Testimonials." If you are a speaker, an "Invite" page is appropriate to let others know the process to book you. An embedded video player or even a simple link to a video you have placed on YouTube can help people connect to you and your message.

No matter the purpose of the site, branding should be consistent with established color scheme and fonts. The site should match other collateral materials. Your graphics and photos should have consistent styling and your logo should be prominent.

My preference is to avoid pages that scroll for eternity. Always consider how many people will view your site from a smart phone. What fits in a screen capture? If it doesn't fit, consider making a button to click if interested rather than the need to scroll and read, scroll and read. The site should be easy on the eyes. A little movement is interesting—flashing graphics and the once vogue intro video could keep people from lingering. These things may be cool, but they take time to load and our attention span is short. If you want people to stay and browse, or better yet, decide you are a resource to return to, make sure your content offers value, is informative, and interesting. Blogs and links to related or relevant sites are a good strategy to keep people coming back.

Consider how your site looks on multiple browsers. Have you checked it out on Firefox, Safari, Explorer, and Chrome? Did you see how it functions on a tablet or smart phone? If you are offering downloadable PDFs, it is nice to offer a link to download the Acrobat PDF Reader for free. You don't want people to have to leave your site to utilize your content.

Affiliate marketing through your website also has potential. In essence you help a business by promoting their product, service, or site, and they reward you with a commission. There are pros and cons, of course. In my opinion, this is not "easy money." To make money as an affiliate requires high traffic and high volume. You categorize yourself by what you link to. Trust is a key component of building a business. Affiliate marketing is essentially an endorsement—a referral with an actual link encouraging your customers (and friends) to buy.

If the company you link to uses "hard sell" to persuade, if the product is low quality, or the service elicits low satisfaction you will own the negatives of their experience. Affiliate marketing may be a smart move for you if the company is reputable and the product or service you are linking to fits with your core mission and message. If not, affiliate marketing can actually hurt your reputation and water down your brand. I caution you to engage this strategy with your eyes wide open and perform due diligence before signing up.

As you begin to reach out to your niche and beyond, you must remain vigilant to manage your brand. Your reputation, your ideas, and the intellectual property you are marketing are being watched. People are looking and listening. They want you to be the real deal. You have to be the real deal.

Social Media

Over the past few years, social media has grown in a phenomenal way. Facebook, Twitter, YouTube, Google+, LinkedIn, Pinterest ... the list goes on and on. Social networking sites dominate the Internet with huge amounts of traffic. Social media is an innovative, culturally relevant tool to connect to your audience and interact with them in dynamic ways. It helps you keep your finger on the pulse of what interests them and respond to trends as they emerge.

Keeping up with what's hot could be a full time job. Ignore it and you miss a powerful marketing tool. Obsess over it and you focus on sound bytes, followers, and likes—staking your brand on snapshots instead of the big picture.

I am in favor of social media. I have seen it used powerfully and effectively. With a little investment of time and energy, you can learn to use this medium to build your business. If that isn't for you, then there are companies abounding who will gladly manage it for you. It is worth doing. It is worth linking your social media to your website and vice versa. It is a great way to stay in touch. Which social media sites and how many you want to engage with is your choice. Learn about it. Experiment with it. You will be glad you did.

eMail Marketing

No doubt you have received email from people whose mailing list you subscribed to in exchange for a discount or promotion. Maybe you have experienced the joy of having your email address sold to an aggressive marketing company who turned around and sold it to someone else, resulting in unwanted junk mail you must sort through daily to get to the mail you actually want to read.

So if everyone hates junk mail, why engage? Why collect email addresses and build a list in the first place? If most marketing emails are not opened, or if they are they aren't given a serious read, why bother? Because email marketing works. It continues to be an inexpensive, effective way to get your message out. Sales specials, new product offerings, and fresh approaches to your message can all be advertised to those on your email list.

I recommend that mass emails be short, visually stimulating, and not ALWAYS trying to sell something. In fact, sending out short, motivational communication or "how to" tips regularly (though not so often as to be annoying) is a great way to connect to your market.

If your emails are enjoyable or useful, they will be opened and read regularly, so when you do make a sales pitch, it will receive attention. If every email is designed to sell, you can count on them being sent to the junk folder.

No doubt you have been to a market with people in the aisles handing out samples. There are always people browsing who take advantage of a free lunch, not intending to buy anything. So why do the companies spend money on handing out samples of their product? Why are they giving it away? Because samples work. People like to try before they buy and there are so many things to choose from. You must grab people's attention and be memorable if you are to rise above the competition. Putting your message in front of people in bite-sized "screen-capture" pieces is good strategy.

I subscribed to Seth Godin's daily email blog and got his short messages for some time before purchasing his books. Those little bits of wisdom made me hungry for more of what he had to say. The sample worked! I now look for titles he has written before I browse for other authors I do not know.

There are lots of email marketing services out there to meet your ambition and your budget. Give it a try. Connect with people. Give away some things for free. Offer a discount if they respond within a prescribed time period. Send out useful information with no strings attached. Ask for your subscriber's opinions—then listen to what they have to say.

Keep the emails short. We ran an experiment for a client by splitting his contact list. We sent half a short email and the other half a longer, more descriptive email. Both carried the same subject line and both advertised the same thing. At the close of the message, there was a button asking the reader to click and watch a short video. The open rate for the long and short emails was statistically even. However, the response rate to the short email (meaning the reader clicked the button and watched the video) was almost 50% higher!

Don't be afraid to explore new avenues for marketing your mind. You might be surprised to find an unlikely client taps into your world because you took that extra step.

A Final Note of Marketing

Marketing in its simplest form is telling people what you have to offer. It doesn't have to be slick or slippery. It can be honest and sincere. You can never be completely removed from a marketing perspective if you intend to stay in business or extend your ministry. If you fail to continue marketing after you have closed a sale or completed a contract, you may not have continuing business.

A lot of intentional effort goes into marketing your mind. You must work hard to publish your book or create a video series. Your effort will be great, and your team will labor together to pull you through. Here's a suggestion that comes from my heart. Once you cross the finish line, celebrate the victory! Celebrate with the people who believed in you and supported you in the process. But don't stop with your team. Extend your delight to those who have embraced your message. Show some gratitude. It will go a long way toward keeping you at the top of their list, and it will fill your own heart with joy.

Respond with Gratitude

On a broader scale, it is important to thank people who have entrusted you with their business. Let customers know you appreciate the opportunity for their business. Say thank you. You can do this with a telephone call, an email, a card, or a gift. People will be pleased to know you appreciate them.

Another way you might encourage them is to offer repeat customers discounts because of their loyalty. A small discount is a relatively small price to pay for a customer who repeatedly uses your service or embraces your message. It doesn't really matter how you say thank you, only that you actually communicate your gratitude.

Saying thank you may be seen by some as just another marketing strategy. It is much more. It is certainly good business. More importantly, it is the right thing to do. It is one of the first lessons we were taught as children and its value will never diminish. Say thank you.

So, let me express my gratitude to you. Thank you for taking the time to read this book. Thank you for allowing me to express my passion for providing success for others. I may never meet you and be able to personally express my gratitude for reading this material, but know that your willingness to come to this page touches my heart and blesses my soul.

Committed to your success,

Wendy

Wendy K. Walters

Part Three Summary

Reaching people with your message requires:

◆ Telling others what you have to offer

◆ Telling them where and how they can get it

◆ Telling them why they need to buy it from you

Identifying your niche is a powerful tool.

◆ Listen to yourself. What are your specific areas of interest and expertise? What problems are you passionate about and uniquely equipped to solve.

◆ Listen to others. What needs or desires do they express? What questions do they have that you are positioned to answer?

◆ Find your "Blue Ocean"—determine what makes you special and different. What makes you a distinct alternative?

Marketing your message by connecting directly with people is powerful. We discussed three strategies:

◆ Relationship Marketing

◆ Referrals

◆ Endorsement Marketing

◆ All these strategies require you to be authentic
   and credible. Being genuinely interested in
   people is not a gimmick—it is a demonstration
   of your character and core values.

**Marketing to the masses requires devices that go beyond
your ability to maintain a personal touch. We touched on the
following strategies:**

◆ Having a well designed website with easy
   navigation and the ability to order products

◆ Use of social media (blogging as well)

◆ Use of eMail marketing

Conclusion:

◆ Marketing your mind is hard work. You can do it. You
   must remain focused and dedicated to the process.

◆ Celebrate victories with your team and
   those who supported you through the
   process—demonstrate your gratitude.

◆ Extend your appreciation to those who engage in
   your services or buy your products. Always say
   thank you and live with generosity of spirit.

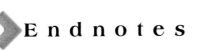

Endnotes

Chapter One

1. Proverbs 22:1 AMP *(emphasis added)*
2. Proverbs 22:1 The Message *(emphasis added)*
3. 2 Corinthians 9:8-12 NKJV
4. Proverbs 3:3-4 NLT *(emphasis added)*
5. Psalms 112:6-8 The Message *(emphasis added)*

Chapter Six

1. Romans 12:3 The Message

Chapter Eight

1. Proverbs 11:25 NLT

Chapter Ten

1. Proverbs 27:2 NIV

Chapter Eleven

1. Psalms 92:12 KJV

Success means never letting the competition define you. Instead you have to define yourself based on a point of view you care deeply about.

—Tom Chappell, Tom's Of Maine

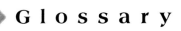

Glossary

Words that are common to the fields of publication and printing, but less well known within the general public have been included for easy reference.

1. **Brand**—distinctive identifying attributes developed by and unique to a specific person, business, or organization, including names, signs, symbols, logos, taglines, color combinations, and slogans.

2. **Copy Editor**—an individual who edits written material to ensure correctness in content, revising a manuscript by checking spelling, adjusting grammar, verifying research, eliminating redundancy and keeping consistency in style.

3. **Copyright**—according to the US Copyright Office FAQ, copyright *"protects original works of authorship including literary, dramatic, musical, and artistic works such as poetry, novels, movies, songs, computer software and architecture. Copyright does not protect facts, ideas, systems, or methods of operation, although it may protect the way these things are expressed."* Copyright is designated by the © symbol.

4. **Copyright Infringement**—is the prohibited and unauthorized use of copyrighted works, included copying, reprinting, or performing such works without the express and documented permission of the owner. Actions which disregard the copyright holder's rights are violations of and are punishable by law.

5. **Content Editor**—an individual who edits written material to add value to content, revising a manuscript by adjusting words, phrases, or subject placement to improve a story line of more clearly define a process.

6. **Format**—the general physical appearance of a book, including the shape and size, number of pages, typeface, binding, quality of paper, margins, organization, style, headings, included graphics and pull-quotes, when appropriate.

7. **Ghost Writer**—an individual, usually a professional writer, who is paid to compose material that is officially credited to another person. Ghost writers are also employed to edit material. Politicians, business executives, and celebrities often choose to use the service of a ghostwriter to write or edit an autobiography or other written material.

8. **ISBN**—a commercial book identification number. The International Standard Book Number is a 13-digit code represented by an EAN 13-digit bar code. This is the familiar bar code found on commercially produced books and other products and scanned at cash registers.

9. **LCCN**—this is the Library of Congress Control Number. This number is assigned by the Library of Congress and is beneficial in providing bibliographic information for book lists and libraries. Any academic or formal reference to your book can be traced to this number.

10. **Plagiarism**—unauthorized use or close imitation of the language and thoughts of another author represented as one's own.

11. **Proofread**—to read and correct mistakes in a written or printed piece of writing.

12. **Proofreader**—an individual whose responsibility it is to proofread material.

13. **Public Domain**—intellectual property not covered by copyright law, or properties of which copyright has expired or those rights have been forfeited. Public domain refers primarily to information, invention, or works which are publically available, and intangible to private ownership, and/or those which are available for use by members of the public.

14. **Pull-Quote**—also known as a lift-out quote, is an excerpt or a quotation, usually printed on the same page as the excerpt. In most instances it employs a larger or perhaps a different typeface and serves to draw a reader into the topic or to emphasize a particular point.

15. **Revision**—the process of changing a written document or other printed, visual, or spoken media to reflect changes in substance, style, grammar, and punctuation. Revision is also applied to subsequent printings of books which have been updated since their original publication.

16. **Service Mark**—a trademark symbol relating to services rather than products. The service mark is designated by using the ^{SM} symbol.

17. **Trade Mark**—The US Patent and Trademark Office identifies a trademark as *"any word, name, symbol, or device, or any combination, used, or intended to be used, in commerce to identify and distinguish the goods of one manufacturer or seller from goods manufactured or sold by others, and to indicate the source of the goods. In short, a trademark is a brand name."* A trademark that is not legally registered is designated by the symbol ™. A registered trademark is designated by the ® symbol.

Meet the Author

Wendy K. Walters has a gift for identifying what makes a person unique and bringing that to the forefront. Like few others, she can guide you through the maze of distinctions that make you stand out—looking better and sharper, maximizing your originality. As a consultant she has helped launch many people's dreams, translating their ideas into profitable businesses.

Author of *Marketing Your Mind, Postworthy—Words to Encourage and Inspire*, and *Intentionality—Live on Purpose!* Wendy has also developed a powerful Branding Profile that recognizes core competencies, pinpoints core values, identifies the problems you are uniquely gifted to solve, helps target your niche market, and develop a signature brand.

As a partner in Palm Tree Productions, Wendy not only coaches people through the process of developing intellectual property, she has the resources available to bring those ideas across the finish line into tangible reality—creating products and platforms for services.

She speaks at conferences and business events, activating and empowering people to declare their dreams, identify with their passion, and create strategic action plans. Wendy points others confidently toward their destiny and encourages them to walk each day with intentionality—living with purpose, on purpose! She finds no greater joy than seeing others released into their potential and living 100% fully alive.

www.wendykwalters.com
www.palmtreeproductions.com

Resources

The *Branding Profile* is an assessment tool created to take you through a process of discovery to identify your "unique factor" and pull out your core competencies, core values, developed skill sets, and areas of mastery. It helps evaluate your intellectual property to target your market and develop a signature brand. Wendy uses this tool with her clients and has now made it available for personal use.

Postworthy—Words to Encourage and Inspire is a compilation of some of Wendy's most inspiring and encouraging posts on social media outlets. Intentional communication is an important component of her recipe for success and this book of motivational quotes will edify and lift you. It makes a delightful gift.

Intentionality—Live on Purpose! helps you participate in the design of your own future. It will help you identify your passion and discover all that makes you unique, then guide you to focus your choices, your resources, and your energy on developing mastery in your field. Rather than being swept along by life's current, you will take the helm of your destiny and step into your unlimited future. You can begin to live fully engaged, fully alive—live with purpose ... on purpose!

Available at:

www.wendykwalters.com

Speaker | Author | Consultant